Accelerate Your Hustle:

Master Startup Game with
7 Rules &
9 Attributes

उध्यमेना हि सिद्धायन्ति कर्यानि ना मनोरथे ।
नाहि सुपतस्य्यो सिंहास्यो प्रबिश्यन्ति मुखे त्रिगा ॥

English Translation:
Success comes from efforts and not from wishful thinking,
A deer doesn't enter a lion's mouth automatically

Dibyendu Choudhury

DIBYENDUCHOUDHURY

Disclaimer

This book is a work of science and art mixed with lessons of Management. Names, characters, places and events and inferences from the Hindu Mythologies and Epics are either the products of the author's imagination or his opinion. Any resemblance to actual persons, living or dead or from Hindu mythologies are purely coincidental. No claim is made regarding the historical or theological accuracy and are either made or implied. Historical, religious, or mythological characters, events or even places are used fictitiously. While adequate care has been taken to respect different religions and ideologies, the characters in this book are representative of differing views in the world today.

Copyright © 2024 Dibyendu Choudhury

All rights reserved, no part of this publication may be reproduced, distributed, or transmitted in any form or by any means, including photocopying, recording or any electronic or mechanical methods, without the prior permission of the author, in case of brief quotations embodied in critical reviews and certain other non-commercial uses permitted by copyright law. For permission requests, write to the author or address given below

Author E-mail: dibchoudhury@gmail.com

Web Site: www.dibyenduchoudhury.com
Twitter: @DibsChoudhury
Facebook: https://www.facebook.com/dibyendu.choudhury.7/

DEDICATION

Dedicated to my Father my first Guru who had been instrumental in teaching and guidance throughout my entire life.

पिता स्वर्गः पिता धर्मः पिता परमकं तपः ।
पितरि प्रीतिमापन्ने सर्वाः प्रीयन्ति देवताः ॥

Transliteration:
pitā svargaḥ pitā dharmaḥ pitā paramakaṃ tapaḥ ।
pitari prītimāpanne sarvāḥ prīyanti devatāḥ ॥

Hindi translation:
मेरे पिता मेरे स्वर्ग हैं, मेरे पिता मेरे धर्म हैं, वे मेरे जीवन की परम तपस्या हैं।
जब वे खुश होते हैं, तब सभी देवता खुश होते हैं !

English translation:
My Father is my heaven, my father is my dharma, he is the ultimate penance of my life. If he is happy, all deities are pleased.

Source: Mahabharata Shanti Parva 258.20

CONTENTS

Preface

Acknowledgments

Chapter1: Introduction

Chapter 2: Cases of failed Indian startups and hustlers

  Failed Startups

    A. Costlier Mistakes to avoid

    B. What happens if Start-up fails?

Rule 1: Building a Customer Obsessed Organization

Rule 2: Solve problems; never try to sell.

Rule 3: Everybody is not your customer.

Rule 4: Spread the Good Words

Rule 5: Don't stay self-employed

Rule 6: Sales Solve All Problems:

Rule 7: Don't Run by Preconceived Notions: The Government of India is One of the Largest VCs for Funding.

Chapter 3: Mindset

  Attribute A: Self-Reflection

  Attribute B: Assess Skills and Knowledge

  Attribute C: Seek Feedback

  Attribute D: Setting of Goals

Attribute E: Identify values and passions
　　Attribute F: Taking Assessments
　　Attribute G: Seek Learning Opportunities
　　Attribute H: Tracking Progress
　　Attribute I: Patience and persistence
Web References

PREFACE

I was drawn to the initial setbacks faced by two Indian startups, Byju and Paytm, which revealed a pattern of inflexibility and shortsightedness in a dynamic market. The Amazon Mini TV series "Hustlers" provided a fresh perspective on entrepreneurship, inspiring the creation of this book.

Starting a venture with innovative ideas backed by disruptive technologies has become an appealing career path for India's tech-savvy youth, offering an alternative to traditional employment in large multinationals. However, it can also lead to missed opportunities and potential job losses. While entrepreneurship offers unique opportunities for personal and professional growth, it also comes with risks and challenges that can impact lives.

The experiences of Paytm and Byju highlight the importance of governance, compliance, and transparency in business. Articles from Moneycontrol, MSN, Forbes India, and others emphasize the need for good governance practices within companies.

The recent struggles of star startups like Byju's, Theranos, China Evergrande, Paytm, and WeWork underscore the importance of integrity and transparency in business practices. Pressure from investors and regulatory bodies has led to depreciation in Byju's valuation and a decline in Paytm's stock price, raising concerns about the sustainability of their models and the leadership of their founders.

Both Byju's and Paytm have faced challenges from competitors and regulators, resulting in significant financial losses and reputational damage. The ability of their founders, Raveendran and Sharma, to navigate these challenges and restore their companies' success remains to be seen.

Many entrepreneurs, including Elizabeth Holmes, Adam Neumann, and Hui Ka Yan, have faced the consequences of unchecked ambition and unethical practices. Despite early success, these individuals failed to recognize warning signs of impending failure.

Founders who become disconnected from reality and isolate themselves from constructive criticism risk alienating their employees, customers, and stakeholders. To avoid this, founders must challenge their assumptions, seek diverse perspectives, and remain open to feedback.

Similar mistakes have occurred in the music industry when one member's ego overshadowed the group dynamic, leading to disbandment. Collaboration is crucial, and founders must recognize when one member's dominance threatens the group's cohesion.

In conclusion, entrepreneurs must learn from failure, prioritize ethical decision-making, and remain adaptable to succeed in today's competitive market. **"Accelerate Your Hustle: Master Startup Game with 7 Rules and 9 Attributes"** is a comprehensive guide for entrepreneurs seeking to start and sustain a successful business in India's dynamic economy. It offers practical advice and real-life examples, covering various aspects of entrepreneurship, from idea validation to scaling a business effectively. The term "hustler" embodies the spirit of modern entrepreneurship, emphasizing resilience, adaptability, and a relentless drive for success.

Dr. Dibyendu Choudhury

Date: Sunday, 14 April 2024

ACKNOWLEDGMENTS

Acknowledgment

I extend my heartfelt gratitude to you, dear reader, for embarking on this journey with me. This book is not a mere theoretical or academic treatise; it is a practical and actionable guide. Drawing from my own experiences as a teacher, trainer, and mentor to numerous entrepreneurs and intrapreneurs in India, I aim to provide insights that resonate with the real challenges faced in the Startups for the Hustlers.

Within these pages, you'll find case studies featuring some of the most successful and influential business leaders in emerging India. But this book isn't just about celebrating triumphs; it also delves into enterprises that stumbled and failed to take flight. It's a candid exploration of the entrepreneurial landscape, where dreams collide with reality, and resilience becomes the cornerstone of success.

For the Young Trailblazers

This book is tailored for the young and ambitious souls who seek to steer their lives toward entrepreneurship. Aspiring hustlers, take note: I encourage you to invest in your own startup, nurture it over the next decade as its CEO, and build an enterprise fueled by innovative technologies. In doing so, you'll not only shape your destiny but also provide opportunities for the educated youth eager to carve their careers in the startup ecosystem.

Why startups, you ask? Because the near future holds a promise—a promise that startups will offer more growth potential than established MNCs. As the tides shift, the entrepreneurial spirit will thrive, and those who dare to dream will lead the charge.

Lessons from the Journey

My father once advised me to start a business fresh out of engineering college. However, I chose a different path—to gain experience through wage employment. Along the way, I seized opportunities to work as an intrapreneur within multinational organizations. My roles spanned sales, business development, and various facets of marketing.

Through mentors, peers, customers, and even competitors, I imbibed invaluable lessons. Notably, my time at the National Institute for MSME (ni-msme) left an indelible mark. Established in 1960, ni-msme shattered the myth that entrepreneurs are exclusively born, revealing that they can also be nurtured through training and mentoring.

Embracing Failures

I've stumbled, made mistakes, and faced failures as an individual. Yet, I clung to my dreams tenaciously. For it is from these failures that true learning emerges—the raw material that shapes our experiences.

A Shared Purpose

As you turn these pages, my hope is that my experiences become your compass. Let us navigate the intricate landscape of Indian Startup business together. Whether you're a budding entrepreneur or an aspiring intrapreneur, I'm here to share insights, unravel complexities, and guide you toward your goals and ambitions.

Ready to Begin?

Dear reader, are you ready? Let us embark on this transformative journey—one that promises growth, resilience, and the thrill of creating something remarkable.

With anticipation,

Dr. Dibyendu Choudhury

P.S: For any comments or clarifications the author can be reached anytime through his website

www.dibyenduchoudhury.com

CHAPTER1: INTRODUCTION

I was in the process of authoring a book about the MSME sickness in India, which was a natural progression from my previous book, "How to Start a Business in India: Idea to Implementation." However, without finishing the book on MSME Sickness, I began inquisitive about the failures of two recent start-ups in India, Byju and Paytm. You may also be curious about the cause of the demise of Paytm and Byju, two of India's largest Unicorns. That sounds like an intriguing and timely topic. Simultaneously, I observed an Amazon Mini TV series called "Hustlers" which became the inspiration for authoring this book. I dove into the research, uncovering the assorted reasons behind the downfall of these once-thriving companies called Unicorns. As I continued to explore the intricacies of the business world, I realized that there was a common thread linking these failures: a lack of adaptability and foresight in a dynamic market. The Amazon Mini TV series "Hustlers" provided me with a fresh perspective on entrepreneurship and served as a catalyst for my book on challenges to Indian businesses in today's dynamic landscape. This book aims to shed light on the pitfalls that entrepreneurs must avoid in order to thrive in the competitive world of business.

We live in a time of life-changing ideas, which should come as no surprise to inquisitive students, researchers, and entrepreneurs. If an idea exists, it can be developed into a proof-of-concept, for which all engineering institutions/universities/management colleges act as incubators. Once a VC accepts your proof of concept, obtaining startup funding is simple. Slowly, the concept can emerge, and the company can raise Series A, B, and C capital ahead of its IPO. Start-ups should aim for an initial public offering. The entire game centres around developing value propositions and perceived valuations. Today, there are many venture capitalists in India eager to invest in creative ventures. Because "Shark Tank" and similar shows are getting more popular in India, it is reasonable to anticipate a high number of people seeking private financing and pursuing entrepreneurship as a vocation.

Though "starting up" is a fantastic way to be rewarded in a variety of ways, you will miss receiving better job offers and careers from many MNCs, whereas others must work for at least 5-10 years to obtain a stable and sustainable position in the sector. However, you will reach a much higher horizon and launch your own venture within these 5-10 years. When compared to pursuing rewarding employment, the potential return is far greater than that of launching a start-up. You become your own boss. You have the freedom to make decisions and implement strategies that align with your vision and goals. Additionally, the satisfaction of building something from the ground up and seeing it succeed is unparalleled. While the risks are high, the rewards can be even higher. Entrepreneurship offers a unique opportunity for personal and professional growth that can be incredibly fulfilling in the long run.

However, what I wrote in the preceding paragraph is not as lovely as it appears. Some precautions must be taken. It has the potential to endanger many lives by speeding up the expansion of unnecessary grids. Remember that "haste" to become famous and wealthy quickly may "waste" your career and endanger the lives of many other young people linked with you.

After conducting comprehensive research, I came across various articles that detail the challenges and controversies faced by Paytm and Byju. According to Moneycontrol, these firms may have suffered as a result of their founders' success and the accolades they received while ignoring governance, compliance, and transparency problems. MSN also explores the founders' personality traits and leadership styles, demonstrating how they may have contributed to their companies' failures. Forbes India examines how weak corporate governance harms firms and why independent directors and auditors must be held accountable. Overall, the success and fame of founders sometimes overshadows the importance of good governance practices in a company. The articles shed light on the potential consequences of neglecting these crucial aspects and serve as a reminder for other entrepreneurs to prioritize transparency and accountability in their own businesses. The founders must strike a balance between ambition and responsibility to ensure success and sustainability of their companies in the long-run.

The Fall of Star Startups Creating a market leader such as Byju's, Theranos, China Evergrande, Paytm, or WeWork requires exceptional talent. However, it appeared to me that some companies suffered as a result of their founders' remarkable success and early fame. This led to a lack of oversight and accountability, resulting in their downfall. By focusing solely on growth and expansion without considering the ethical and financial implications of their decisions, these once-promising startups crumbled under the weight of their own hubris. The cautionary tales of these fallen giants serve as a wake-up call to all entrepreneurs to prioritize integrity and transparency in their business practices to avoid a similar fate.

Investors and regulatory bodies are currently applying pressure on two prominent Indian startups: Think & Learn Private Limited, the parent company of EdTech giant Byju's, and One 97 Communications Ltd, which operates FinTech platform Paytm. Byju Raveendran and Vijay Shekhar Sharma, the founders of these companies, are among numerous entrepreneurs whose ambitious visions may have adversely impacted their ventures. Byju's valuation, once at $22 billion two years ago, has significantly depreciated, while regulatory issues surrounding Paytm Payments Bank have led to a roughly 40% decline in the company's stock price following operational restrictions imposed by the Reserve Bank of India. These setbacks have raised questions about the sustainability of the business models employed by these startups as well as the leadership capabilities of their founders. Both Byju's and Paytm have faced challenges from competitors and regulatory authorities, leading to significant financial losses and reputational damage. It remains to be seen whether Raveendran and Sharma can navigate these turbulent times and steer their companies back to success.

This is the fate of many aspiring entrepreneurs who become sidetracked by the thrill of initial success. In the United States, Elizabeth Holmes, the founder of Theranos, and formerly the country's youngest and wealthiest self-made millionaire, is serving an 11-year jail sentence for scamming investors with her fraudulent blood-testing company. Last year saw the downfall of yet another billionaire entrepreneur, Adam Neumann, whose venture WeWork faced failure, alongside Sam Bankman-Fried's bitcoin exchange FTX, which was impacted while he was incarcerated. Hui Ka Yan was once a business celebrity in China after establishing a real estate empire that transformed rural communities into metropolitan hubs where middle-class Chinese could buy homes. It propelled Hui into the ranks of the country's most powerful and wealthiest men. Hui is currently facing corruption charges following the bankruptcy of his venture, Evergrande, while the towns he built remain abandoned, a sign of China's economic crisis. Hui's downfall is sudden and dramatic, with many questioning his business practices and the sustainability of his empire. The corruption charges against him have tarnished his reputation and left many investors and homeowners in turmoil. The abandoned towns serve as a stark reminder of the risks and consequences of unchecked growth and unchecked power in China's economy. Hui's story is a cautionary tale of the dangers of unchecked ambition and the importance of ethical business practices.

Raveendran, Sharma, Holmes, and Hui are all creators, both men and women, with the vision and will to make their dreams a reality. Starting and growing a company to multibillion-dollar valuation is no easy task. It is estimated that 99% of the startups fail by the second year. It requires extraordinary ability to not only survive but become market leaders like Byju's or WeWork. These people, including Hui, overcome countless hardships and barriers on their path to achievement. Aspiring entrepreneurs must learn from their failures and prioritize ethical decision-making to avoid the negative consequences of unbridled development and power. Entrepreneurs who recognize the value of ethical business practices can build long-term, profitable companies that benefit both themselves and society as a whole.

So, what went wrong derailing the efforts and bringing such thriving firms to a halt? Until recently, Raveendran enjoyed unwavering support from financial backers, private equity firms, and the public. Holmes' board of directors boasted figures such as Henry Kissinger and the former US Secretary of State George Shultz. However, the charisma of the young woman who aspired to be a female Steve Jobs captivated these notable figures to such an extent that they neglected to pose fundamental inquiries. As a result, Raveendran and Holmes were able to operate freely, making judgments that led to the demise of their separate businesses. It appears that their early success and image of invincibility blinded people around them to the warning indicators of imminent failure. Finally, unrestrained authority, a lack of accountability, and blind faith in their leadership brought these once-promising firms crumbling down.

That is the issue with founders who grow larger than their companies. They begin to distance themselves from reality live in a bubble. The same self-assurance propelling the initial success will foster the illusion that they can do no wrong. In the process, they ignore or quiet any opposition, creating an echo chamber for themselves. This echo chamber shields them from constructive criticism and prevents them from seeing the potential pitfalls that lie ahead. As a result, they become disconnected from the very people they are supposed to serve their employees, customers, and stakeholders. Their downfall is not just a consequence of their own hubris but also a failure in recognizing the importance of humility and self-awareness in leadership. In order to prevent a similar fate, founders must constantly challenge their own assumptions, seek diverse perspectives, and remain open to feedback, no matter how uncomfortable it may be. Only then can they truly lead their companies to sustainable success. There is a saying that in the downfall of such large companies, the working professionals and their livelihood suffer. Entrepreneurs and investors do not suffer; they get their money out. However, the employees who dedicated their time and effort to these companies are left jobless and often struggle to find new opportunities in a competitive market. Entrepreneurs should remember the human cost of their decisions and to prioritize the well-being of their employees above all else. Integrity and transparency will not only thrive businesses, but the individuals who contribute to their success will also be protected in the event of a downfall. This lesson is a crucial reminder that success should never come at the expense of others' livelihoods.

Not only have entrepreneurial ventures suffered due to such misconceptions, but the music industry also bears witness to bands disbanding when one member insists on exclusive attention. Groups like the Beatles, Pink Floyd, Pearl Jam, and Eagles parted ways when a member began to perceive themselves as superior. Rolling Stone magazine, in a feature titled 'The Biggest, Messiest Band Breakups in Music History,' quoted U2 representative Bono, who remarked, "Your worth is measured by the recognition you garner, but eventually, when individuals thrive, egos tend to seek dominance." He enjoys being the king of the castle, which is when things begin to go apart. Egos get in the way, and the music becomes secondary to personal goals. It's regrettable when talented musicians allow their pride to obstruct the creation of something truly original together. Collaboration is essential in the realm of music, and when one member begins to overpower the others, the magic fades. Many bands have learned this lesson the hard way throughout history.

Likewise, founders and CEOs of companies often tend to attribute all their initial success solely to the abilities of self, disregarding the significance of timing or luck. If you liked it, ask a few questions thus far.

Are you an aspiring entrepreneur?
- Do you think of turning your passion into a profitable and long-term,

sustainable business?
- Do you want to learn the best practices and challenges of India's startup ecosystem?
- If you answered yes to any of the preceding questions, then you picked the right book. "Hustle Smarter in India: From Startup to Success" is an extensive manual on beginning and running a profitable and long-term business in one of the world's most dynamic and diverse economies. Whether you're at the conceptual, prototyping, or product stage, this book will help you explore the issues and opportunities in the Indian startup ecosystem, with a focus on the Government of India, one of the largest VCs that these failed entrepreneurs have never approached or funded. With practical advice and real-life examples, "Hustle Smarter in India" delves into the intricacies of navigating the regulatory landscape, building a dedicated team, securing funding, and scaling your business effectively. By understanding the unique challenges and advantages of operating in India, entrepreneurs can position themselves for success and avoid common pitfalls outlined in the

seven rules and ten attributes. Do not miss this essential guide for anyone looking to thrive in the vibrant and competitive startup scene of India.

Now the question comes: Who are these "Hustlers"?

According to the Internet, the term "hustlers" refers to people who are extremely motivated, ambitious, and determined to achieve their goals, often via hard effort, tenacity, and innovative problem-solving. Hustlers are noted for their inventiveness, resilience, and desire to seize chances and overcome challenges in order to succeed.

In popular culture and colloquial usage, "hustlers" can also refer to people who participate in unorthodox or entrepreneurial activities to make money, such as street sellers, freelancers, independent contractors, or small business owners. These folks may strive diligently to make ends meet, pursue their interests, or attain financial independence outside of typical employment frameworks. Overall, the term "hustlers" conveys ideas of ambition, drive, and initiative, and it is frequently used to characterize people who are prepared to hustle or work hard in order to attain their goals and create opportunities for themselves.

In today's quickly changing market, the classic definition of an "entrepreneur" has evolved into that of a "hustler." With technological breakthroughs propelling us into the era of smart technologies, where our TVs are now Smart TVs and our mobile phones are Smart Phones, it is important to update our nomenclature for today's business executives. These modern entrepreneurs must not only possess innovative ideas and strategic thinking, but also the relentless drive and tenacity to hustle in order to stay ahead in the competitive market. The ability to adapt to innovative technologies and navigate the rapidly changing business landscape is essential for success in today's digital age. As such, the term "hustler" accurately captures the essence of the modern entrepreneur, who is constantly hustling to seize new opportunities and drive their business forward.

Entrepreneurship is no longer limited to traditional business models or industries. Today's entrepreneurs are more than just risk-takers and inventors; they are strategic hustlers capable of navigating complex markets and capitalizing on opportunities in a quickly changing digital world. As technology continues to disrupt industries and affect consumer behaviour, the entrepreneur's role has evolved to encompass a broader set of talents and attributes. Today's entrepreneurs are constantly striving to remain ahead of the curve, from employing data analytics to inform decision-making to harnessing social media and digital marketing to build brands. The term "hustler" encapsulates the spirit of resilience, adaptability, and unwavering pursuit of success that distinguishes modern entrepreneurs. It represents an agile and resourceful mindset, with challenges viewed as opportunities and setbacks as learning experiences. In this new era of entrepreneurship, where innovation and disruption are the norm, embracing the hustler persona is more than a choice; it is a must. It is about accepting change, seizing opportunities, and persistently seeking excellence in order to achieve entrepreneurial greatness.

This book will help you learn:

- How to validate your idea and determine product-market fit

- How to create a lean, agile team and culture

- How to raise finances and persuade investors.

- How to take advantage of the gig economy and freelancing.

- How to promote and sell your goods or service

- How to handle regulatory, legal, and ethical

challenges.

- How to Scale and Expand Your Startup

- Learn from the success stories and failures of Indian startups.

"Hustle Smarter in India" is not just a book. It serves as a blueprint, toolbox, and mentor for your business path. It is realized and understood by talking with several professionals and practitioners who have done it successfully before. It contains insights, recommendations, and case studies that will motivate and enable you to hustle smarter and achieve your startup goals.

CHAPTER-2

IF IT WAS EASY, EVERYONE WOULD DO IT

STORIES OF FAILED INDIAN STARTUPS.

17 FAILED INDIAN STARTUP'S CASE STUDIES

@dibyenduchoudhury

CHAPTER 2: CASES OF FAILED INDIAN STARTUPS AND HUSTLERS

FAILED STARTUPS

Every day, hundreds of new startups emerge in India. Many fails because they avoid learning from the triumphs of other firms that have reached the top. Here are 17 unsuccessful Indian businesses, along with analyses of why they failed and what their founders said. These anecdotes are cautionary tales for aspiring entrepreneurs, showing frequent difficulties and mistakes to avoid. By investigating the causes of their failures, aspiring entrepreneurs might get vital insights into what it takes to thrive in the competitive Indian market. Readers can benefit from these studies and interviews by learning from the mistakes of others and applying these lessons to their own enterprises, enhancing their chances of developing a successful enterprise. For example, one business might have failed amid poor market research and understanding of consumer preferences, leading to a mismatch between products and demand. Another could have faced challenges in securing funding or effectively managing cash flow, resulting in financial difficulties that ultimately led to closure. These real-life examples provide valuable lessons in areas such as strategic planning, financial management, and market analysis that can help entrepreneurs understand the complexities existing in the Indian business landscape and avoid common pitfalls.

1) Dazo

Dazo, a food-tech start-up that emerged as a "food on demand" company, based in Bangalore, failed due to fierce competition and a lack of funding. Despite initially gaining traction with customers, Dazo struggled to differentiate itself in a saturated market and failed to secure the necessary capital to sustain its operations. The company, unable to manage its finances and adapt to the dynamic market conditions, ultimately witnessed its downfall. This is a reminder of the importance of strategic planning and financial management in securing the sustained success of a business in India's dynamic and competitive business environment.

Start-up Details:

- Founders: Monica Rastogi, Shashaank Shekhar Singhal
- Industry: Food & Beverage
- Started in: 2015
- Closed in: 2016
- Number of employees: 10–50
- Funding Amount: No Data
- Primary reason for failure: competition

2) Frankly

Frankly.me, a social platform for Q&A was unable to raise the much-needed funding, leading to its shut down. This highlights the crucial role that securing adequate funding plays in the sustainability of a business, especially in a rapidly evolving market like India. Without the necessary financial backing, even innovative startups with potential like Frankly.me can struggle to survive. It underscores the need for entrepreneurs to carefully assess their financial needs and develop a robust strategy for securing funding to support their growth and success in the competitive business landscape.

Start-up Details:

- Founders: Abhishek Gupta, Nikunj Jain
- Industry: Social Media
- Started in: 2014
- Closed in: 2016
- No of employees: 50-100
- Funding Amount: < $1M
- Primary reason for failure: Lack of PMF

3) HotelsAroundYou

HotelsAroundYou, an India platform for short and last-minute bookings had to shut down as they failed to raise more money. This highlights how important it is to achieving product-market fit to attract further funding and sustain business operations. Despite the initial promise and potential of HotelsAroundYou, the inability to secure additional funding ultimately led to its closure in 2016. Abhishek Gupta and Nikunj Jain, the founders of HotelsAroundYou, likely learned valuable lessons about the challenges of scaling a startup without a solid foundation of financial support.

Start-up Details:

- Founders: Animesh Chaudhary, Harsha Nallur, Mohsin Dingankar
- Industry: Travel
- Started in: 2013
- Closed in: 2017
- Number of employees: 1–10
- Funding Amount: < $1M
- Primary reason for failure: competition

4) Koinex

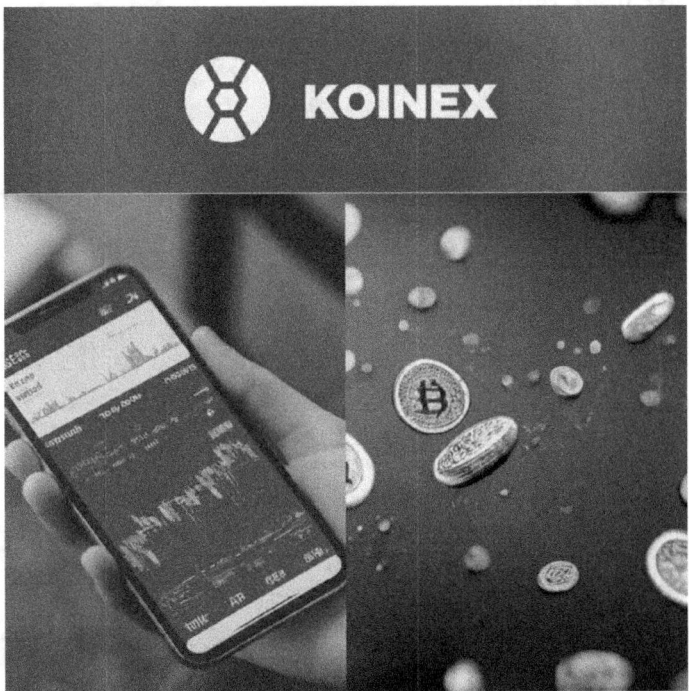

Koinex, an Indian cryptocurrency exchange platform, faced the harshness from India's laws against cryptocurrencies, and other obstacles like little profits lading to its shut down. It was established by Rahul

Raj and Aditya Naik in 2017, when the cryptocurrency market in India was booming. However, regulatory challenges and the lack of clear guidelines for operating a cryptocurrency exchange in the country proved to be major hurdles for Koinex. Despite their efforts to navigate the legal landscape, the platform was forced to shut down in 2019. The founders, like many others in the industry, faced the harsh reality of trying to operate within a regulatory framework that was not yet ready to embrace the potential of cryptocurrencies.

Start-up Details:

- Founders: Aditya Naik, Rahul Raj, Rakesh Yadav
- Industry: Finances
- Started in:2017
- Closed in: 2019
- Number of employees: 50-100
- Funding Amount: No Data
- Primary reason for failure: legal challenges

5) Lumos

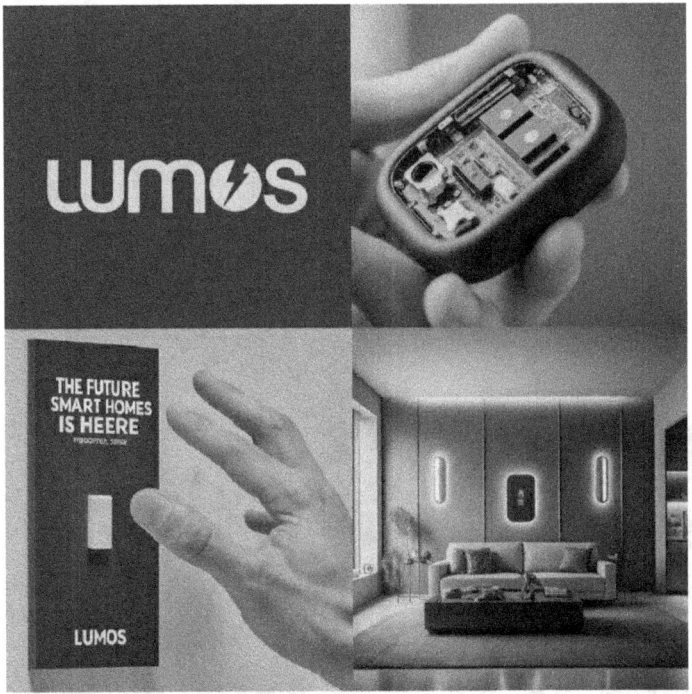

Lumos was established to provide smart switching technology. Following the closure, the founders acknowledged that they were not the suitable team to establish a hardware company. They decided to pivot and focus on developing software solutions for the financial industry instead. Despite the challenges they faced with Lumos, the founders remained resilient and determined to be successful in the ever-evolving world of technology and innovation. Their experience with Lumos taught them valuable lessons about the importance of adapting and being flexible in the face of adversity.

Start-up Details:

- Founders: Pritesh Sankhe, Tarkeshwar Singh, Yash Kotak
- Industry:Software & Hardware
- Started in:2014
- Closed in:2015
- Numbers of employees: 1–10
- Funding Amount: No Data
- Primary reason for failure: lack of experience

6) PepperTap

PepperTap was an online platform for buying groceries from the local markets. Customers considered the delivery fees expensive, and ultimately the start-up was shut down. Navneet Singh and Milind Sharma were responsible for founding PepperTap in 2014. The startup quickly gained popularity among customers looking for a convenient way to shop for groceries online. However, the high delivery fees charged by PepperTap ultimately led to its downfall, as customers found more cost-effective alternatives. Despite its short-lived success, PepperTap is a lesson for startups to carefully consider their pricing strategies and understand their target market's needs.

Start-up Details:

- Founders: Milind Sharma, Navneet Singh
- Industry: Food & Beverage
- Started in: 2014
- Closed in: 2016
- Number of employees: 1,000-5,000
- Funding Amount: > $50M
- Primary reason for failure: Poor Product

7) RoomsTonite

RoomsTonite, an app developed to book hotels at the last-minute for the people visiting India, raised $1.5M in funding but the money didn't arrive and it was shut down. RoomsTonite, like PepperTap, serves as a cautionary tale for startups in the tech industry. Despite its promising concept and initial funding, the failure of RoomsTonite highlights the importance of securing financial backing and managing cash flow effectively. The unexpected closure of the app underscores the unpredictable nature of the startup ecosystem and the need for contingency plans in place. Startups should learn from the mistakes of companies like RoomsTonite and PepperTap to avoid similar pitfalls and ensure long-term success in a competitive market.

Start-up Details:

- Founders: Suresh John
- Industry: Travel
- Started in:2014
- Closed in:2017
- Number of employees: 100-250
- Funding Amount: $1M-$10M
- Primary reason for failure: lack of funds

8) SchoolGennie

SchoolGennie, that once provided solutions by saving time, reducing costs, and helping schools to make better decisions, didn't test the product-market fit. As a result, SchoolGennie struggled could not attract or retain customers, leading to a decline in revenue and ultimately, their closure in 2018. Their failure is a lesson for startups to thoroughly test their product-market fit before scaling up operations. By conducting market research and gathering feedback from potential customers, startups can better understand their target audience and increase their chances of success in the competitive business world. It is essential for startups to be proactive in identifying potential pitfalls and having contingency plans in place to navigate challenges effectively.

Start-up Details:

- Founders: Amit Gupta, Pardeep Goyal
- Industry: Education

- Started in:2013
- Closed in:2014
- Number of employees:1-10
- Funding Amount: $0
- Primary reason for failure: lack of experience.

9) Stayzilla

Stayzilla, formerly a prosperous homestay network backed by $33.5M in funding, shuttered its operations due to unsustainability in operational expenses and financial deficits. This highlights the importance of proper financial planning and management in ensuring the longevity of a startup. By learning from the mistakes of failed ventures like Stayzilla, aspiring entrepreneurs can better prepare themselves for the challenges of the competitive business world and increase their chances of success.

Start-up Details:

- Founders: Rupal Yogendra, Sachit Singhi, Sachit Singhi, Yogendra Vasupal

- Industry: Travel
- Started in: 2005
- Closed in: 2017
- Number of employees: 250-500
- Funding Amount: $10M-$50M
- Primary reason for failure: lack of focus

10) Zoomo

Zoomo aimed to instill trust within the Indian used car market, which was still in its nascent stages. However, it eventually decided to cease operations. This closure likely stemmed from a lack of emphasis on cultivating and sustaining trust within the market, which is vital for a platform dealing with significant transactions like used cars. By examining the setbacks of enterprises like Stayzilla and Zoomo, entrepreneurs can glean crucial insights into the significance of maintaining focus on core business objectives and strategies. It's evident that without a dedicated effort to build trust and provide value to customers, even well-funded startups may struggle to thrive in the fiercely competitive business landscape.

Start-up:

- Founders: Arnav Kumar, Himangshu Hazarika
- Industry: Transportation
- Started in: 2014
- Closed in: 2016
- Number of employees: 10–50
- Funding Amount: $1M-$10M
- Primary reason for failure: bad business model

11) Adleaf Technologies

Chetan Vashistth, founded "Adleaf Technologies" in 2013, which offered programming bootcamps as well as software solutions. While the business initially thrived, it eventually succumbed to a series of poor business decisions and inadequate financial management. Despite Chetan Vashistth's innovative vision, the lack of a robust business model contributed to the downfall of Adleaf Technologies. The closure of the company serves as a stark reminder for entrepreneurs about the critical importance of strategic planning and financial prudence in navigating the competitive business landscape.

Start-up Details:

- Founder: Chetan Vashistth
- Industry: Education
- Started in: 2013
- Closed in: 2014
- Funding Amount: $0
- Primary reason for failure: mismanagement of funds

12) Autto.in

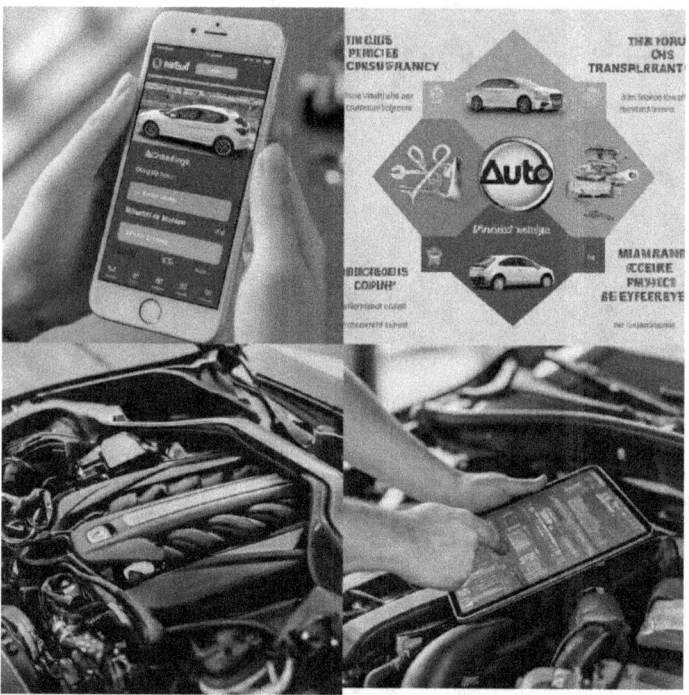

Deepak founded Autto.in in 2017, an on-demand doorstep car service provider. Shortly after its launch, a co-founder joined him, and together they initiated the marketing efforts of the start-up, investing heavily in customer acquisition. As funds dwindled, they sought out investors who exerted pressure on them to scale rapidly. Eventually, after a few months, they made the decision to close down the business. Despite their initial success in marketing the startup, Autto.in ultimately faced financial instability due to excessive spending on customer acquisition and pressure from investors to grow rapidly. This mismanagement of funds, combined with the inability to sustain growth, led to the decision to shut down the business. This serves as a cautionary tale for entrepreneurs about the importance of financial planning and stability in the competitive business world.

Start-up Details:

- Founder: Deepak Murthy
- Industry: Transportation
- Started in: 2017
- Closed in: 2017
- Funding Amount: < $100K
- Primary reason for failure: lack of funds

13) FreshConnect

Co-established by Tarun, Freshconnect was an online B2B marketplace specializing in fresh agricultural produce. However, due to errors like lack of focus and subpar hiring decisions, they failed to secure a funding round. Ultimately, another company acquired them. This experience taught Tarun to focus on the core business goals and making sure to hire the right team members. Despite the initial setbacks, Tarun was able to learn valuable lessons about financial planning and stability in the competitive business world. This ultimately helped him navigate future ventures more successfully and avoid the same fate as his first startup.

Start-up Details:

- Founder: Tarun Gupta
- Industry: e-Commerce
- Started in:2018
- Closed in:2020
- Funding Amount:$0
- Primary reason for failure:Bad Management

14) InoVVorX

InoVVorX operated as an app development firm, catering to clients while also pursuing internal projects. Initially successful, with a team of 25 members, generating $300k in service revenue, and securing $100k in funding, the company's ambition to pursue numerous internal projects led to excessive spending and eventual closure. Following InoVVorX's demise, Tarun Gupta gleaned essential insights on the significance of maintaining a focused business strategy and avoiding resource overextension. With this newfound knowledge, he is determined to approach his next venture with more caution and discipline. By avoiding the mistakes of his previous startup, Tarun hopes to build a successful e-commerce business that will thrive in a competitive market.

Start-up Details:
- Founder: Maxim Dsouza
- Industry: Software and Hardware
- Started in: 2010
- Closed in: 2016
- Funding Amount: $100K-$500K
- Primary reason for failure: Lack of funds

15) Jobridge

Jasmeet, an Indian software engineer, started a venture a few years ago to innovate revenue strategies for his business directory. He developed a job board with a distinctive offline-online model. However, their concept was ahead of its time, and coupled with a flawed business model, they ultimately had to cease operations. Now, with a fresh perspective and past experience, Jasmeet is determined to create a successful platform that will revolutionize the job search process. By focusing on a more sustainable business model and adapting to the current market trends, Jasmeet believes that Jobridge 2.0 will be a game-changer in the industry. With a drive for innovation and a commitment to success, Jasmeet is ready to take on the challenge of building a thriving e-commerce business that will withstand the test of time.

Start-up Details:
- Founder: Jasmeet Singh
- Industry: Software & Hardware
- Started in: 2017
- Closed in: 2017
- Funding Amount: $0
- Primary reason for failure: Bad Business Model

16) Mishra Motors

Mishra Motors, a venture started with an aim to be the premier electric sports bike in India collapsed due to time and capital. Mishra Motors was founded by a team of passionate individuals with a vision to revolutionize the electric sports bike industry in

India. Unfortunately, despite initial excitement and interest from investors, the startup ultimately faced challenges with timing and capital. As a result, Mishra Motors was unable to overcome these obstacles and ultimately closed its doors. This serves as a reminder of the importance of proper planning and financial management in the start-up ecosystem.

Start-up Details:

- Founder: Naveen Mishra
- Industry: Transportation
- Started in: 2014
- Closed in: 2016
- Funding Amount: $0
- Primary reason for failure: Lack of Funds

17) The Punjab Kitchen

Amit, a dedicated sales professional, made the decision to establish a home-cooked food business alongside his wife. They initially invested $1,200 per month to kickstart the startup and attract their first customers. However, upon launching, they encountered a significant challenge: their competitors offered substantially lower prices. Despite attempts to pivot, they eventually made the difficult decision to close the business. Proper planning and financial management are crucial in the world of startups, as evidenced by the story of Naveen Mishra's failed transportation startup. The Punjab Kitchen, founded by Amit, also faced challenges due to market competition and pricing issues. Despite their initial investment and hard work, the business ultimately could not compete and had to be closed down. This highlights the importance of an effective market research and staying adaptable in the face of challenges for startup success.

Start-up Details:

- Founder: Amit Gogia

- Industry: Food & Beverage
- Started in: 2014
- Closed in: 2015
- Funding Amount: $0
- Primary reason for failure: Competition

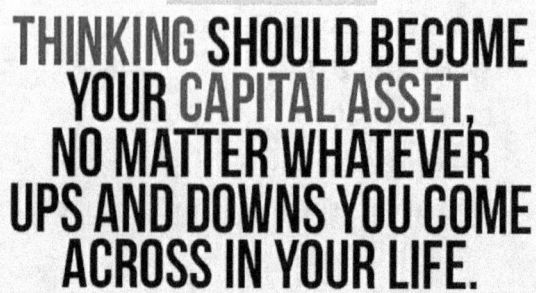

Chapter -3

CASES OF FAILED INDIAN STARTUPS AND HUSTLERS?

CHAPTER 3: WHAT HAPPENS TO FAILED STARTUPS AND HUSTLERS?

A. Costlier Mistakes to avoid

After the initial excitement and adrenaline of starting a new venture wear off, many entrepreneurs are left grappling with the harsh reality of failure. The path of entrepreneurship is littered with failed startups and hustlers who gave it their all but couldn't quite make it work. So, what happens to these individuals after the dust settles and the business closes its doors?

For some, the experience serves as a valuable lesson, teaching them important skills and providing insights that they can apply to future endeavors. Others may struggle with feelings of disappointment and uncertainty about their next steps. Some may choose to pivot and try again with a new idea, while others may decide to pursue a different career path altogether. Regardless of the outcome, the journey of entrepreneurship is often filled with ups and downs, and it is how individuals choose to respond to failure that ultimately shapes their future success. It is important to remember that failure is not the end, but rather a stepping stone towards future growth and success. Those who can learn from their mistakes and adapt will ultimately be the ones who come out stronger on the other side. It is during times of struggle that true resilience and determination are tested, and those who can persevere despite setbacks are the ones who will eventually find their way to success. Considering failure as learning instead of a defeat is the key to achieve goals in the world of entrepreneurship.

By considering failure as an opportunity for learning and development, entrepreneurs can cultivate a growth mindset, enabling them to emerge stronger after setbacks. This capacity to adapt and thrive amidst challenges distinguishes successful entrepreneurs. Rather than allowing setbacks to hinder their progress, they harness them as motivation to propel themselves closer to their objectives. In the fast-paced and ever-changing world of entrepreneurship, the ability to embrace failure and turn it into a positive learning experience is a valuable skill that can lead to long-term success. For example, a tech startup may face a setback when their latest product launch fails to gain traction in the market. Instead of giving up, the entrepreneurs behind the startup analyze what went wrong, gather feedback from customers, and use that information to make improvements for their next iteration. This growth mindset allows them to pivot their strategy, innovate, and ultimately achieve success by creating a product that meets the needs of their target market.

The journey of building and expanding a startup is challenging. Despite meticulous planning and preparation, unforeseen mistakes and obstacles are inevitable. While we may assume that successful business owners operate with flawless precision, even the most prominent entrepreneurs encounter errors from time to time. Thus, making mistakes is an inherent aspect of any entrepreneurial journey. However, certain mistakes can prove to be particularly costly for startups, inflicting significant damage. Nevertheless, amidst failures, resilient entrepreneurs emerge, leveraging setbacks as opportunities to learn, adjust, and flourish.

Here are some success stories:

upGrad: Mayank Kumar and Phalgun Kompalli founded upGrad, which stresses quick decision-making. Their agility and adaptability have helped them achieve success in EdTech sector.

Zomato: Despite initial difficulties, Zomato persisted. Its creators, Deepinder Goyal and Pankaj Chaddah, grew it from a restaurant finding website to a global food-tech behemoth.

Ola: Ola's Bhavish Aggarwal and Ankit Bhati faced stiff competition from Uber yet persisted. Ola is currently a household name in the ride-hailing industry.

Failed startups and determined hustlers are two sides of the same entrepreneurial coin. While failure teaches us humility, success stories encourage us to keep going. In India's startup ecosystem, both failure and resilience contribute to the dynamic tapestry of invention and progress. Entrepreneurs like Goyal, Chaddah, Aggarwal, and Bhati embody the spirit of perseverance and resilience that is vital for success in the unpredictable world of startups. Despite facing challenges and setbacks, they remained steadfast in their pursuit of innovation and growth. Their stories serve as inspiration for aspiring entrepreneurs and a reminder that determination and hard work can lead to great achievements in the ever-evolving landscape of business.

The Biggest and Most Expensive Mistakes Entrepreneurs Make in Startups

1. Not hiring competent team in the initial phases
2. Over dilution of equity
3. Being comfortable post success
4. Being cheap
5. Rushing and forcing progress
6. Entering into partnerships
7. Trying multiple things simultaneously
8. Stressing due to negative outcomes
9. Inflexible vision
10. Investing in professional branding prematurely

Many entrepreneurs acknowledge making costly mistakes during their start-up journeys. These errors have provided invaluable lessons, contributing to their growth and eventual success. It's crucial for aspiring entrepreneurs to heed these experiences, avoiding the same costly missteps. By remaining vigilant against these potential pitfalls and taking proactive measures to circumvent them, entrepreneurs can enhance their prospects of establishing a thriving and enduring business in today's ever-changing business landscape.

Learning from the Top Entrepreneurs: Key Lessons on Avoiding Costly Mistakes in Startups

Mistakes are not created on purpose; they simply happen. It could be due to poor decisions, judgments, or a move at inappropriate time. Entrepreneurs often consider their early startup blunders to be their most significant. They may have underestimated market demand, overextend their resources, or failed to adapt to changing trends. However, learning from these mistakes can be invaluable in shaping future strategies and avoiding similar pitfalls in the future. By acknowledging and analyzing past errors, entrepreneurs can develop a stronger sense of resilience and adaptability, ultimately becoming more successful in their ventures.

Let us learn about the most expensive mistakes by entrepreneurs in detail:

1. **Not hiring competent team in the initial phases**

In the initial phase, entrepreneurs make a mistake by not prioritizing proper team development. Failure to hire smarter people sooner stifles a startup's growth and success. This mistake results in a lack of diverse skill sets and perspectives, which are crucial for problem-solving and innovation. With a weak team in place, entrepreneurs struggle to keep up with the demands of a rapidly evolving market. By hiring smart individuals early on, entrepreneurs can set their ventures up for long-term success and growth. The team that achieves the objective is equally important as the goal itself. Entrepreneurs are usually so focused on their objectives that they fail to watch out for talented people. This tiny inaccuracy proves to be highly costly over time.

2. Over dilution of equity

One more common mistake is that founders become overly generous with their ownership. Equity is an asset to be maintained and it should not be taken for granted. Many entrepreneurs admitted that this was their most significant mistake in the early years. They were quick to give away shares to early employees or advisors without considering the long-term implications. With the progress of company, these early decisions can come back to haunt them, leading to power struggles and disagreements over the direction of the business. It is essential for founders to carefully consider the value of equity and only distribute it to those who truly deserve it and are committed to the long-term success of the venture. By being more strategic and thoughtful about equity distribution, founders can avoid potential pitfalls and ensure a stronger foundation for their company's future growth. So, rather than giving up equity in employee equity pool, it's important to save it for the right time. Sam Parr, the creator of "The Hustle," one of the most successful media businesses in America, admitted that being overly generous with ownership was his biggest mistake early on.

3. Being comfortable post success

Another common fault is getting too comfortable after gaining success. When entrepreneurs experience their newfound prosperity, they either feel motivated or become comfortable. Sam Parr fell into the trap of getting too comfortable after experiencing early success with The Hustle. Instead of continuing to push himself and his team to innovate and grow, he became complacent with the success they had achieved. This lack of drive and ambition ultimately hindered the company's potential for further growth and expansion. It serves as a valuable lesson for entrepreneurs to never rest on their laurels and always strive for continuous improvement and evolution in their businesses. Being comfortable may be advantageous for some time, which may eventually become expensive. An entrepreneur may generate a year's worth of money in a single month and simply get comfortable with it. However, decelerating afterwards would be a costly mistake for the startup's future.

4. Being Cheap

Entrepreneurs in the early phases of a startup frequently feel they can manage everything alone while saving money. This can turn out to be a serious mistake because it lowers work quality and loses time, the most valuable resource. By trying to cut corners and save money, entrepreneurs may end up sacrificing the long-term success and growth of their business. Investing in resources and expertise that can help the business thrive and reach its full potential is very important. By being cheap, entrepreneurs may miss out on opportunities for growth and innovation, ultimately hindering the evolution of their business. To stay competitive and continue improving, entrepreneurs should invest in the necessary tools and expertise, even if it requires spending more money upfront. Instead of cutting costs every time, firms must spend the money wisely in order to get true help from experienced engineers, designers, and others. Distributing the workload among trained personnel ensures high-quality labor and enhanced earning possibilities.

5. Rushing and forcing progress

This is a typical error that everyone makes. The market is extremely competitive, and in order to stay up, entrepreneurs may tend to rush and force things, which may work at the moment, and may prove the statement "Haste makes waste" in the long run.

While the impact of this mistake may not be obvious right away, it can cause future challenges. Working fast and forcibly might be the most costly blunder for entrepreneurs. Therefore, entrepreneurs should prioritize quality over speed. By ensuring that all tasks are completed to a high standard, they can avoid costly mistakes and setbacks in the future. Additionally, focusing on quality work can lead to enhanced earning possibilities, as customers are more likely to trust and recommend a business that consistently delivers excellent products or services. Ultimately, patience and attention to detail are key factors in the success of any startup.

6. Entering into partnerships

This is a common mistake made by entrepreneurs in their enterprises. The entrepreneurial journey can be lonely. Entrepreneurs often bring on a partner or a co-founder as a means of support.

It is usually preferable to work with the known and trustworthy people. Having someone unknown causes disagreements and lack of trust, eventually jeopardizing the viability of any startup. Many entrepreneurs say this was a costly error they made when starting their businesses. Finding the right partner is crucial for the growth and stability of a startup. It is necessary to choose potential partners ensuring that they share the same vision and values as you do. This will help to avoid any conflicts or disagreements down the line and will ultimately contribute to the success of the business. Remember, a strong partnership can make all the difference in the world of entrepreneurship.

7. Trying multiple things simultaneously

Entrepreneurs exhibit multitasking abilities. However, many consider this as a costly mistake for startups. Entrepreneurs address too many issues at once, which stops them from focusing on a single goal.

The most essential thing is to have the main objective in mind and take steps along the way. However, when entrepreneurs focus on multiple things, they become sidetracked from their main purpose, resulting in a costly mistake. Entrepreneurs should prioritize and focus on one goal at a time to avoid becoming overwhelmed and losing sight of their main objective. By addressing multiple issues simultaneously, entrepreneurs risk spreading themselves too thin and hindering their progress. Instead, they should concentrate on the most critical tasks that will directly contribute to the success of their business. This focused approach will help them stay on track and make more informed decisions, ultimately leading to a more successful and sustainable business in the long run.

8. Stressing due to negative outcomes

Overly worrying about unfavourable outcomes is another costly error that business owners make. Many entrepreneurs consider this as a serious mistake as it demoralizes them leading to even more negative consequences.

It's crucial for individuals to acknowledge, embrace, and glean lessons from their mistakes rather than fixating on them excessively. Overwhelming stress can lead to distractions, fatigue, and costly errors in startup ventures. Had Elon Musk dwelled on the setbacks of his electric vehicle project, he may not have maintained his position at the forefront of innovation today. Entrepreneurs must cultivate a positive mindset, prioritizing problem-solving over ruminating on failures. By leveraging lessons learned and forging ahead with determination, success remains attainable. Elon Musk's resilience and unwavering focus on his objectives, despite obstacles, underscore the significance of maintaining optimism in the face of adversity. Ultimately, it is important that entrepreneurs remain resilient and not let fear of failure hold them back from achieving their full potential.

9. Inflexible vision

Another common mistake by entrepreneurs is being overly inflexible with their vision and goals. Entrepreneurship requires constant learning. To have a vision is crucial, but failing to be adaptable along the way is a costly mistake for any startup.

Managing a startup requires ongoing talks, identifying new market trends, understanding users, and incorporating feedback. Neglecting to validate transitions and maintaining inflexibility ultimately leads to stagnation. Entrepreneurs must understand that adaptability and openness to change are vital for the success of their business. Embracing new ideas and pivoting when necessary can lead to innovation and growth. By staying flexible and open-minded, entrepreneurs can navigate difficulties and setbacks confidently, ultimately leading to a more sustainable and successful business venture. In conclusion, a rigid vision can hinder progress and limit potential opportunities, while adaptability and resilience are key traits for thriving in the ever-evolving world of entrepreneurship.

10. Investing in professional branding prematurely

Another major and costly mistake by entrepreneurs is engaging in professional branding before the startup is ready for it. While branding is critical for establishing a market presence, investing too much in the early stages can deplete the money needed for future growth.

Going for professional branding in the initial phase can be a significant gamble that could pay off handsomely or become a terrible and costly mistake for a business. Therefore, entrepreneurs should carefully assess their business's readiness for professional branding before making any significant investments. It is essential to build a solid foundation and establish a strong product-market fit before diving into branding efforts. This approach will ensure that resources are allocated effectively and efficiently, setting the business up for long-term success and growth. By prioritizing timing and strategic planning, entrepreneurs can avoid the pitfalls of premature professional branding and instead position their startup for sustainable success in the competitive business landscape.

Conclusion

A startup's path has its ups and downs. There are days when we celebrate our successes and days when we lament them. No matter how well the team and systems work, there is always the possibility of some missteps along the way.

The aforementioned are the most serious and costly mistakes made by entrepreneurs. One may learn from the mistakes and strive to prevent them, because great entrepreneurs are those who not only make mistakes but also learn to cope with them. By learning from these mistakes, entrepreneurs can better position their startups for sustainable success in the competitive business landscape. It is important for entrepreneurs to stay resilient and adaptable with challenges, as the path to success is not smooth all the time. By acknowledging and learning from their mistakes, entrepreneurs can grow and improve their business strategies, ultimately achieving long-term success. Great entrepreneurs face setbacks with grace and determination, using them as learning opportunities to propel their business forward. They recognize that failure is an inherent aspect of the entrepreneurial path and leverage it as inspiration to innovate and progress. Through fostering a positive outlook and welcoming challenges, entrepreneurs can establish a robust groundwork for their startups to flourish in the dynamic market landscape.

THE MASTER HAS FAILED MORE TIMES THAN THE BEGINNER HAS EVEN TRIED.

What happens if Start-up fails?

@dibyenduchoudhury

B. WHAT HAPPENS IF START-UP FAILS?

This is the million-dollar question: what happens when a startup fails. When a firm fails, the consequences can be devastating for the founders, workers, investors, and other stakeholders. The money losses can be enormous, but the emotional cost can be considerably higher. However, many successful businesses have faced failure before finding success. It is critical to learn from past failures, pivot when needed, and move forward with newfound determination and resilience. Failure is never the end of the path, it is a stepping stone to greater achievement.

The outcome for founders can vary widely. In some cases, founders may end up facing financial difficulties and may even go broke. This can happen if the founders have invested a considerable amount of their own money into the startup or have taken on personal debt to finance the business. Additionally, if the startup has raised funding from investors, the founders may be personally liable for some of the debt if the business cannot repay it. However, for those who are able to weather the storm and learn from mistakes, failure can ultimately lead to greater opportunities and achievements. They may pivot their business model, seek out new investors, or even start fresh with a different venture. Experience of failure can also provide valuable lessons in resilience, adaptability, and resourcefulness, applicable to future endeavors. Ultimately, the path towards success is rarely smooth, and setbacks and failures are a part of the journey towards achieving one's goals.

Always remember that not all founders end up broke when their startup fails. In some cases, founders may have taken steps to protect their personal finances, such as setting up the business as a separate legal entity (such as a corporation or limited liability company) to shield their personal assets from business debts. Additionally, some founders may have saved money or made wise investments with their earnings from the startup, allowing them to weather the failure without facing financial ruin. It is pivotal to approach entrepreneurship with a sense of resilience and preparedness for any obstacles that may come your way. Remember, failure is never the end of the road but is a stepping stone to future success. By taking proactive steps to safeguard your personal finances and making smart financial choices, you can navigate the good and bad phases of startup with confidence and determination. Staying focused on the long-term goals and trust in your abilities will help you overcome challenges along the way.

In terms of financial success, entrepreneurs of unsuccessful firms have a lower chance. While there are clearly cases of founders who have achieved great success following a failed venture, the reality is that, majority of the unsuccessful startups do not result in large financial advantages for the owners. For example, a founder who properly manages their personal finances may have saved enough money to pay living expenses for a while after their firm fails, allowing them to reorganize and pursue new opportunities. However, absent a successful exit or acquisition, most failed company founders' chances of making a fortune are minimal. However, knowledge gained by creating a firm, even if it fails, can be beneficial and lead to future chances. The lessons learned from the failure can be transferred to future ventures, making the founder more resilient and seasoned in the field of entrepreneurship. Furthermore, the contacts and ties formed during the startup process may lead to future partnerships and collaborations. So, while the cash gains may not be immediate or significant, the intangible benefits of having a start-up can have a long-term impact on the founder's career and personal development. It is stated that once an entrepreneur, always an entrepreneur.

Overall, the outcome for founders of unsuccessful firms is determined by a number of factors, including their financial status, business structure, and ability to recover from loss. While some founders may struggle financially, others go on to new endeavors and eventually succeed.

So, what happens when a start-up fails?

Institutional investors, not crowdfunding investors, are the primary investors in this context. The founder's financial stability depends on the business stage. At the pre-seed stage, the founder may not receive compensation for their efforts, but at the seed stage, they can sell off some equity. At the Series A stage, the founder may have to give up more control of the company in order to attract larger investments. If the startup ultimately fails, the founder may face personal financial losses and have to start over from scratch. However, many successful entrepreneurs have experienced failure before finding success, using their past experiences to learn and grow in their future endeavors.

Another side, because most founders invest their own money at the outset, it is frequently reported as debt. They receive partial or full repayment of their obligation. Also, when the company progressed from seed to Series A and further, the founders' salaries began to approach the industry benchmark for hiring a CEO. If a hired CEO for that level of firm should make Rs.4.0 lakhs (INR 400,000) per month, the founder can earn between 50 and 80% of that, or whatever the board agrees on. Remember that investors want their investees to generate enough money to focus on the firm and avoid side hustles. This ensures that the founders are fully committed to the success of the company and are not distracted by other sources of income. It also aligns their interests with those of the investors, as they are motivated to grow the business and increase its profitability. Ultimately, the founders' salaries are a reflection of the value they bring to a start-up, and the level of responsibility they hold in driving its success.

Furthermore, a smart Hustler would have started shifting some of their liquid capital to other endeavors like real estate and startups. Founders are unlikely to go bankrupt during the seed stage due to various factors. One of the main reasons for this is the fact that they are usually very careful with how they manage their personal finances, understanding the risks involved in starting a new business. Additionally, many founders have an effective network of supporters and mentors to provide guidance and financial assistance if needed. Overall, the financial stability of the founders during the seed stage of any start-up is crucial for the company's success in the long run.

Now, what happens when a funded business goes down?

During investment, the investment thesis, term sheets, and agreements often show the "Rights of First Refusal," and the shares sold are not often "ordinary shares." The shares sold to investors are called "Preference Shares." Preference shares typically come with certain rights and privileges, such as priority in receiving dividends or assets in the event of liquidation. This implies that if a funded business goes down, investors holding preference shares may have more protection and potential for recovering their investment compared to holders of ordinary shares.

Which means if anything happened to the business and it had to wind down, the preference shareholders have to get paid from the money recovered from sales of assets, etc. This will start from the earliest investors who are yet to exit, to the last investors in that order. This hierarchy ensures that preference shareholders are prioritized when it is about recouping their investment. This can be reassuring for investors, as it provides a level of security and protection to them. However, it is important for investors to carefully consider the terms and conditions of preference shares before investing, as these can vary and may impact the level of protection they receive.

Often, in the case of winding down, a portion of the customer losses are anticipated to be compensated before investors withdraw their assets. Regardless of what happens during this process, the founder is paid last, and investors may lose money. Often, they should come away with "nothing" from the pool. This structure ensures that investors are prioritized in terms of receiving compensation in the event of a company winding down. It also highlights the importance of due diligence and understanding the risks of investing in preference shares. Ultimately, while preference shares can offer a level of security, investors must be prepared for the possibility of losing their investment in certain circumstances. Investors should carefully assess their risk tolerance and financial goals before making any investment decisions involving preference shares.

However, if the fault is not at the founder's end, the board (of which the founder should be a nominee) may opt to award the founders a percentage of the wind-down proceeds. However, if the shareholder agreement initially specifies that the founder would own some shares as preference shares (which isn't ideal), the founder may also eventually become affluent. This can provide some level of protection for the founder in case of wind-down. It is important for founders to carefully consider the terms of their shareholder agreement and the possible consequences of owning preference shares. While there is a possibility of losing their investment, founders may also stand to benefit if the company becomes successful and their preferred shares increase in value. Ultimately, founders should weigh the risks and rewards before deciding to invest in preference shares. If a business goes public or is listed on a stock exchange, such as WeWork, the founder will always be wealthy as they have already cashed out on equity sales and have money in the bank. Due to the lack of IPOs in Africa, this scenario may not be applicable. NGX does, however, have many publicly traded enterprises.

So I'll assume the first few scenarios are correct. Fundraising and winding down an enterprise are more difficult and distressing than I have portrayed here. It is a lengthy and messy legal process that should always be avoided, as it is the worst possible consequence. Therefore, it is essential for founders to carefully consider their options and plan for the future prospects of their businesses. While being listed on a stock exchange can bring wealth and success, it also comes with its own set of challenges and risks. In Africa, where IPOs are less common, founders must be strategic in their decision-making and seek out alternative methods of fundraising and exit strategies. Ultimately, proper planning and preparation can mitigate the difficulties and uncertainties coming with winding down a business.

As I was writing this chapter, I realized that I needed to provide some insights into the process in order to encourage more entrepreneurs to consider hustling as a more viable option. We'd be better off if we knew ahead of time what would happen if the hustle failed. Every day at work, I contact a huge number of entrepreneurs, notably microentrepreneurs, who have already gotten initial funding for their firms from the government or other sources but believe they need to expand but do not have finances for branding and marketing. The bulk of them are unaware that there are three more tiers of funding that will dilute their shares as well as stress. To address this issue, I have been working on creating a comprehensive guide that outlines the various funding options available to entrepreneurs at different stages of their business. By providing them with this information, I hope to empower these microentrepreneurs to make informed decisions about their funding needs and avoid unnecessary dilution of their shares. Ultimately, my goal is to help these entrepreneurs succeed in their ventures, contributing to the growth of our economy.

Then what's the formula to succeed?

After interacting with over 1300 company founders at T-Hub in Hyderabad and several other incubators throughout India, it was determined that silver bullet for success does not exist. However, there are eight laws and ten qualities of a hustler that contribute to success. The following section of this book will go over these eight rules and ten qualities of a hustler that will reduce the danger of failure because entrepreneurship is all about a person's mind, and the entire trip is nothing but experience. Success in entrepreneurship is not guaranteed, but by following the eight laws and ten qualities of a hustler, one can greatly enhance their chances of achieving their goals. These guidelines and qualities have been carefully curated based on the experiences of successful company founders and are designed to help aspiring entrepreneurs overcome the challenges of starting and growing a business. By adopting these principles and embodying the qualities of a hustler, individuals can minimize the risks associated with entrepreneurship and create a way for their own success.

Entrepreneurship requires a combination of hard work, determination, and resilience. It is not for the faint of heart, but for those ready to invest the time and effort to turn their dreams a reality. By understanding the eight laws and ten qualities of a hustler, aspiring entrepreneurs can set themselves up and succeed in a competitive and ever-changing business landscape. These guidelines serve as a roadmap for navigating the ups and downs of entrepreneurship, providing a firm foundation for building a successful business. With dedication and perseverance, individuals can defeat the odds and achieve their goals, turning their vision into a thriving reality.

Hustling is always a better career option than searching for jobs in multinational corporations, both financially and in terms of experience, if it is well-planned and carried out with meticulous dedication and hard work. By taking the initiative to start their own business, individuals can control their own destiny and create opportunities for themselves. While the path may be challenging, the rewards of entrepreneurship are substantial, both personally and professionally. The right mindset and work ethic leads to a fulfilling and successful career that surpasses the limitations of working for someone else. Ultimately, the decision to be an entrepreneur can be a transformative and empowering choice that opens up a world of possibilities for those putting in the effort.

It is critical to understand that each person

functions on a distinct timeline throughout their lives. Don't let reading this book make you feel behind schedule. On the contrary, any time is ideal to begin hustling. Immerse yourself in the eight guidelines mentioned here and focus on developing the 10 vital attributes required to embark on this transformative journey. Remember that age or how soon you achieve your goals does not define entrepreneurship success; rather, it is the determination and perseverance you demonstrate along the route. Accept the process and trust that your journey is going just as it should.

As you commence the journey of smart hustling, consider delving into my other book, "Be the Leader, Not a Boss." This book draws inspiration from Hindu mythology and explores 21 unique characteristics that define a true leader. It serves as a valuable companion in your quest for personal and professional growth, offering profound insights and practical wisdom drawn from ancient wisdom and modern leadership principles. Dive into this enriching read and unlock the secrets to becoming a visionary leader in today's dynamic world. With "Be the Leader, Not a Boss," you will learn how to cultivate qualities such as empathy, resilience, and integrity to become a leader that inspires and empowers others. By combining the timeless wisdom of Hindu mythology with contemporary leadership strategies, this book will guide you on a transformative journey towards fulfilling your true potential. Embrace the teachings within its pages and watch as you evolve into a visionary leader who overcomes the challenges of the modern world with grace and authenticity. Trust in the process, and let this book be your trusted companion on your journey to success.

RULE 1: BUILDING A CUSTOMER OBSESSED ORGANIZATION

To do well in today's fast-paced and very competitive market, startups need to focus on the customer. This means giving customers more than they expect and making them happy by solving their problems through goods and services, meet their needs, and add value to their lives. This way of thinking is especially important in India because the market there is very different and complicated, so it needs a more detailed and tailored approach. Let's look at how a few successful companies in India and around the world have made customers the most significant thing in their businesses. Companies like Amazon, Flipkart, and Zomato have all thrived by prioritizing customer satisfaction above all else. By consistently delivering high-quality products and exceptional service, these companies have built a loyal customer base that keeps coming back for more. In a world with multiple choices for consumers than ever before, it is essential for startups to differentiate themselves by providing an outstanding customer experience. By putting the customer first, businesses can not only survive but also thrive in today's competitive market.

One of the most important things you can do to build a customer-obsessed startup is to value customer comments very highly. Start-ups can learn a lot from customer comments about what their customers want, need, and feel, which can help them make their products and services better. The Indian company Swiggy, which delivers food online, is an example of how customer feedback has helped a new business. Swiggy has always paid attention to what its customers want and knows that they want speed, variety, and ease of use. Based on this input, Swiggy has changed its services to meet these needs. For example, it now delivers food within minutes and lets customers see real-time updates on their orders. Because of this, Swiggy has grown very quickly and is now the market leader in food service. Swiggy's focus on customer feedback has not only helped them improve their services but has also allowed them to stay ahead of their competitors. By constantly listening to their customers and adapting to their needs, Swiggy built a loyal base of customers that values their efficiency and convenience. This customer-centric approach has been key to Swiggy's success and has set them apart in the competitive food delivery industry. As a result, Swiggy continues to thrive and expand its reach, offering customers a seamless and enjoyable dining experience.

Personalizing the customer experience is another important thing that makes customers obsessed. Personalization means making sure that any product or service fits the wants, tastes, and habits of each individual customer. Personalization can make customers feel valued and loved, which can make them more loyal and likely repeat the purchase from you. An important Indian startup that has achieved personalization is Flipkart, a huge online store. Based on what customers have looked at and bought in the past, Flipkart has used data analytics to give them unique suggestions and deals. This has made shopping easier and more fun for Flipkart's users and also helped the company make more money. By tailoring their recommendations to each customer, Flipkart has created a personalized shopping experience that keeps customers coming back for more. This focus on personalization has set Flipkart apart from its competitors and solidified its position as a leader in the e-commerce industry. With the success of personalization strategies like those employed by Flipkart, it is evident that understanding and meeting the individual needs of customers is key to driving loyalty and increasing sales in today's market.

Also, good contact with customers is essential for customer obsession. Customers and you can share information and ideas with each other, get to know each other, and trust each other through communication. Communication between startups and customers helps to solve problems quickly and effectively. It can also help build brand trust and stronger relationships with customers. The Indian startup Zomato, which lets you buy food online and find restaurants, has done a great job with communication. Zomato has talked to its users via social media and asked for their opinions. This has helped Zomato quickly respond to customer questions and issues, as well as make customers happier and keep them as customers. By actively engaging with their customers, Zomato has been able to provide better service and improve their platform based on user feedback. This two-way communication has not only helped Zomato address problems efficiently but has also strengthened the bond between the company and customers. As a result, Zomato built a loyal customer base and established itself as a trusted brand in the competitive food delivery industry. Communication is truly key to fostering positive relationships and driving success in the startup world.

Amazon is a great example of a firm that cares about its customers all over the world. Jeff Bezos, the founder of Amazon, is known for considering the customer to be the most important person in the room. He has even left a meeting chair empty to represent the voice of the customer. Focusing on what customers want all the time has helped Amazon to explore new ideas all the time and become a leader in cloud computing and online shopping. Prioritizing the needs and wants of their customers has helped Amazon to continually innovate and expand their services to meet the ever-changing demands of the market. This customer-centric approach has driven their success in the food delivery industry, and also solidified their reputation as a trusted and reliable brand. As other startups look to Amazon as a role model, they too can learn the importance of putting the customer first in order to achieve sustained success and growth.

To sum up, making a company that cares about customers requires knowing their needs inside and out, giving them a personalized experience, and communicating clearly. Companies like

Amazon and Indian companies like Swiggy, Flipkart, and Zomato show how this way of thinking can pave the path for long-term progress. Startups can make money in the long run by building a loyal customer base and considering the customers to be the center of all their decisions and actions. By prioritizing customer satisfaction and constantly striving to meet their needs, companies can build a strong reputation and win trust of their customers. This trust translates into repeat business, positive word-of-mouth referrals, and ultimately, increased profitability. By following in the footsteps of successful companies like Amazon and Indian startups, businesses can create a sustainable model that focuses on the customer first, resulting in long-term success and growth. Ultimately, the key to building a successful company lies in understanding and prioritizing the exact needs of the customer above all else.

Through consistent delivery of high-quality products and services that exceed customer expectations, businesses can foster loyalty and create a positive brand image. This gives a competitive advantage in the market, as satisfied customers will choose that company over its competitors. Additionally, by actively listening to customer feedback and making improvements based on their suggestions, companies can demonstrate their commitment to customer satisfaction and continuous improvement. Alongside driving revenue growth, this customer-centric approach helps to build a strong and loyal customer base that will support the company for years to come. However, in some cases, businesses may prioritize short-term profits over long-term customer satisfaction, leading to a decline in loyalty and a tarnished brand image. If a company consistently ignores or dismisses customer feedback, it can result in frustrated customers who may seek out competitors that better meet their needs. This lack of responsiveness can ultimately erode the company's competitive advantage and hinder its ability to retain customers over a period of time. On the other hand, a company that actively takes customer feedback and implements changes based on the suggestions fosters a sense of trust and loyalty among its customer base. For instance, if a restaurant consistently receives feedback about slow service and takes steps to improve efficiency, customers will return and recommend the establishment to others.

A problem is only a problem if you refuse to look for a solution.

RULE-2

> Create a business that solves a problem.
>
> @dibyenduchoudhury

RULE 2: SOLVE PROBLEMS; NEVER TRY TO SELL.

In a world focused on buying things and making money, "Solve problems, don't sell" stands out as a moral way to manage a business. Always remember customers are already fed-up with too much advertisement bombardments and sells, they're looking for the solutions of their problems. Ensure you're solving their problem than selling him you just another product or services.

Today, consumerism and profit-driven motives often take centre stage, the principle of "Solve problems, don't sell" emerges as a refreshing and morally upright approach to conducting business. In this fast-paced and ad-saturated era, customers are increasingly weary of relentless advertising bombardments and sales pitches. They yearn for more than just another product or service; they seek real solutions to their problems. As a business owner or marketer, it is important to shift your focus from merely pushing products and services to genuinely addressing your customers' needs. By adopting an empathetic mindset, a profound impact on your target audience can be created. So, rather than attempting to sell to them, aspire to solve their problems and fulfil their desires.

When you prioritize solving problems, you demonstrate a genuine concern for the well-being and satisfaction of your customers. You move beyond a transactional relationship and truly connect with their emotions and aspirations. By empathizing with their struggles, you position yourself as a trusted ally who is committed to making a positive difference in their lives. To effectively solve problems, it is necessary to deeply understand your customers and their pain points. Conduct market research, engage in meaningful conversations, and listen attentively to their feedback. By gaining insights into their challenges, you can customize your products or services to meet their specific needs.

Craft your marketing messages and copy in a way that highlights the solutions you offer rather than aggressively promoting your offerings. Illustrate a vibrant scenario where our product or service seamlessly transforms into the solution to their dilemma, easing their burdens and bringing them closer to their desired outcomes. Focus on the transformation your offering can generate in their lives, emphasizing the benefits and value it brings. Moreover, leverage the power of storytelling to connect with your audience on an emotional level. Share authentic narratives of individuals or businesses your solution has helped, illustrating the positive impact you can create. People resonate more with stories that resonate with their experiences and struggles.

Lastly, make it easy for your customers to act and obtain the solution you provide. Clearly communicate the steps they should take, simplify the buying process, and offer exceptional customer support. By removing any barriers or obstacles, you empower your customers to solve their problems effortlessly and forge a long-term relationship with your brand.

In conclusion, "Solve problems, don't sell" serves as a moral compass for running a business in contemporary world. By centering your efforts around understanding and addressing your customers' needs, you position yourself as an ally rather than a salesperson. Through effective communication, empathy, and a genuine desire to make a positive impact, trust, loyalty, and sustainable success can be built. Remember, your customers are seeking solutions, so be the one who provides them.

This theory stresses how important it is to work on the real problems that people and society are facing instead of just trying to sell things. From an Indian point of view, this method fits very well with traditional beliefs and values that put other people's well-being and the greater good first. With its diverse population and rich cultural history, India has known for a long time how important it is to solve problems for the good of society. This approach not only benefits the community as a whole but also helps to build customer trust and loyalty. By focusing on solving problems, businesses in India can create sustainable relationships with the customers and establish a positive reputation in the market. In a country where social responsibility is highly valued, the "Solve Problems, Don't Sell" philosophy aligns perfectly with the ethos of putting others before oneself. Embracing this mindset can lead to not only financial success but also a sense of fulfilment and purpose in the business landscape.

An example of this is the Indian philosophical idea of "Seva," which means "selfless service." Seva tells people to help others without asking for anything in return. It stresses the idea of solving problems to make everyone's life better and less painful. Recently, Indian companies have also started to think about solving problems instead of just selling things. Some companies, like Tata Group, have started projects to help with social and environmental problems, like getting people access to clean water and green energy. Businesses that work to solve these issues not only improve society, but they also build a good reputation for themselves and gain customers' trust. This shift towards social responsibility is not only beneficial for the communities being helped but also for the companies themselves. By actively working to solve problems and improve society, businesses are able to build a positive reputation and gain trust among customers. This, in turn, leads to increased loyalty and ultimately, more success over time. It is inspiring to see companies like Infosys, Wipro, Unilever and Britania all leading the way in using their resources and influence for the greater good. For example, Tata Group has implemented numerous social responsibility initiatives, such as providing clean water access to rural communities and promoting education for underprivileged children. These actions not only benefit those in need but also enhance the company's reputation and attract socially conscious customers who support their mission.

Worldwide, there are many companies that have done very well with the "Solve Problems, Don't Sell" formula. One such company is Novo Nordisk, a Danish one that focuses on diabetes care. Novo Nordisk doesn't just sell insulin; they've also created full programs to educate and support patients, which helps them better handle their situation. This has not only made millions of people's lives better, but it has also made Novo Nordisk a known leader in diabetes care around the world. Finally, the idea behind "Solve Problems, "Don't Sell" is not merely a business strategy; it's also a way of thinking that shows you understand people's wants and values better. By focusing on finding solutions to issues, companies can not only make money but also make the world a better place to live. Novo Nordisk's approach to diabetes care goes beyond just providing insulin; they've also created full programs to educate and support patients, which helps them better handle their situation. This has not only made millions of people's lives better, but it has also made Novo Nordisk a known leader in diabetes care around the world.

Novo Nordisk's commitment to prioritizing the needs of those living with diabetes has set them apart in the healthcare industry. Their dedication to solving problems rather than simply selling products has created a culture of innovation and empathy within the company. This approach has not only resulted in groundbreaking advancements in diabetes care but has also enhanced trust and loyalty among their customers. As a result, Novo Nordisk continues to be a beacon of hope for those affected by diabetes, offering not just products, but solutions that truly make a difference in people's lives.

However, a detailed counterexample could be seen in a pharmaceutical company that prioritizes profits over patient needs, leading to unethical practices such as price gouging on life-saving medications. This approach harms vulnerable populations and also erodes trust in the healthcare industry as a whole, ultimately hindering progress and innovation in addressing critical health issues like diabetes. For example, in 2015, Turing Pharmaceuticals sparked outrage when they increased the price of a life-saving drug, Daraprim, by 5,000%, making it unaffordable for many patients who relied on it. This unethical practice highlighted the dangers of prioritizing profits over patient well-being in the pharmaceutical sector. In response to public backlash, Martin Shkreli, CEO of Turing Pharmaceuticals, faced legal consequences and was ultimately convicted of securities fraud. This case serves as a cautionary tale for pharmaceutical companies to prioritize ethical practices and patient access to essential medications.

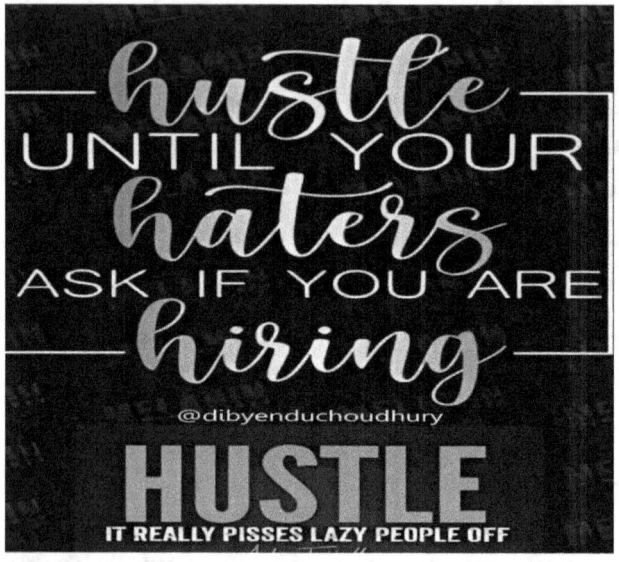

RULE-3
@dibyenduchoudhury

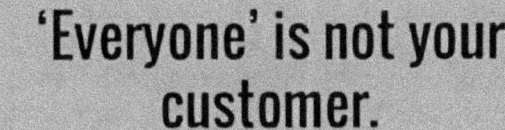

'Everyone' is not your customer.

RULE 3: EVERYBODY IS NOT YOUR CUSTOMER.

Are you a hustler looking to grow your business? Are you tired of feeling constrained by limited resources and ready to explore new horizons? If so, it's time to embrace the potential of expansion. While some may argue that diversifying your business is key for success as a hustler, your focus is on growth, and expansion is your secret weapon. Unlike others, you understand that limited resources should never be seen as an obstacle but rather as an opportunity for innovation and pushing beyond boundaries.

Expanding your business is not about spreading yourself thin or diluting your efforts. Instead, it's a strategic move allowing you to tap into untapped markets, unleash your full potential, and create new avenues for success. By expanding, you open the door to a world of possibilities, where the only limit is your imagination. Imagine the satisfaction of reaching a broader audience, of captivating new customers who are eager to embrace what you have to offer. Picture your business thriving in uncharted territory, leaving your competitors in awe and scrambling to catch up.

More than just about growing your reach; expanding is also about solidifying your position in the market. Every step you take towards expansion strengthens your brand, builds credibility, and establishes your authority as a leader in your industry. Your competitors may fear change, but you thrive on it, using every opportunity to outshine and outperform. Let your ambition guide you as you start this journey of expansion. Fuel your desire to achieve more, to break free from limitations, and to leave a legacy that inspires countless others to follow in your footsteps. This is your moment to seize, your chance to rewrite the rules and reshape the future of your business. Don't let limited resources hold you back any longer. Now is the time to act, to embrace the growth stage strategy of expansion. Unleash your potential, unlock new opportunities, and watch as your business soars to unprecedented heights.

"Not everyone is your customer" is very important in business, especially in the market beyond boundaries, we live in now, where competition is high and customer wants are always changing. This idea says that companies shouldn't try to please everyone. Instead, they should focus on finding out what groups of people they want and what they need, then giving those groups what they want. This is where the option called "identification of Star Customers" comes in. These people are more loyal and bring in more money than other customers. A business owner thinks they are the same as everyone else, but those 20% customers bring in 80% of the profit. This means you should treat them better and run your business for their benefit. It is highly important to find their services and tailor them to them. By understanding and fulfilling the needs of these star customers, a business can increase its overall profitability and success. This also helps build a strong and loyal customer base that will continue to support the business in the long run. By focusing on these key customers, a business ensures that their efforts are directed towards those who will bring in the most revenue and help sustain the business in the future. Ultimately, prioritizing the needs of Star customers leads to a more efficient and profitable business model.

People in India really connect with this idea because Indian society is very diverse and complicated, and it's very important to satisfy the needs and wants of all the different groups of people. India is hard for companies that want to reach a large group of people because it has so many different cultures, languages, and traditions. One big example is the food industry, where businesses like Haldiram's have done well by catering to the different tastes of people from different parts of India regarding food. By understanding and catering to the diverse preferences of customers in India, businesses can establish a loyal base of customers and increase their market share. This approach leads to higher sales and profits, and also helps build a positive brand image. Companies like Haldiram's have set a successful precedent by adapting their products to suit the varied tastes of customers across different regions of India. This customer-focused strategy has proven to be essential for businesses looking to thrive in the Indian market.

Haldiram's has built a loyal customer base all over the country by providing a broad range of products to suit different tastes. "Not Everyone is Your Customer" is an idea that is shown around the world by companies like Apple. Even though Apple is a huge tech company, it has focused on making high-end goods for a specific group of individuals who care about design, innovation, and the user experience. This focused approach has not only helped Apple build a strong brand, but it has also let it charge high prices and keep customers coming back.

"Not Everyone is Your Customer" is a thought worth using in marketing tactics as well as product offerings. For example, the Indian company Zomato first aimed its online food delivery service at tech-savvy city dwellers, knowing that this group was more likely to use such a service. With this focused approach,

Zomato was able to hold a prominent position in the market before expanding to other groups. This strategy allowed Zomato to establish itself as a leader in this industry before attempting to reach a broader audience. By catering to the requirements and preferences of a specific target market, companies like Apple and Zomato created loyal customer bases and were able to command premium prices for their products and services. This focused approach not only helps in building brand recognition but also ensures customer satisfaction and retention in the long run. For example, Apple initially targeted tech-savvy individuals with its high-end and innovative products, like iPhone and MacBook. By consistently delivering quality products and services to this niche market, Apple was able to create a strong brand following and a premium pricing strategy. With this approach, Apple could maintain a loyal customer base and lead the technology industry for years.

In addition to targeting a specific market segment, companies can also differentiate themselves by offering outstanding customer service and support. By providing personalized assistance and addressing customer needs promptly, businesses can enhance the overall customer experience and build long-lasting relationships. This customer centric approach can lead to increased customer loyalty, favourable word-of-mouth referrals, and ultimately, higher profitability. Additionally, companies can differentiate themselves by investing in research and development to continuously improve their products and stay ahead of their competitors. By consistently innovating and adapting to changing market trends, businesses can gain competitive edge and attract new customers while retaining existing ones.

Furthermore, by staying proactive and responsive to customer feedback, companies can address concerns quickly, showing customers that their satisfaction is a top priority. This level of attentiveness earns trust and loyal customers, leading to repeat business and a positive reputation in the marketplace. In today's dynamic business conditions, it is important for companies to prioritize customer satisfaction and continually strive to exceed expectations. With this, businesses position themselves for long-term success and sustainable growth.

To sum up, the idea of "Not Everyone is Your Customer" stresses how important it is to realize the different wants and needs of different groups of customers. Realizing that not everyone will be interested in their goods or services lets companies focus on those who are, which leads to more success and happy customers with time.

A company that focuses solely on one specific demographic and ignores the needs and wants of other potential customer groups could be a detailed counterexample. By alienating these other groups, the company may limit its growth potential and miss out on valuable opportunities for expansion. Additionally, this narrow focus may lead to customer dissatisfaction among those outside the targeted demographic, ultimately hindering long-term success and sustainable growth. In contrast, companies that prioritize inclusivity and diversity in their target audience can target a wider range of customers and tap into new markets. By understanding and addressing the needs of various demographics, these companies can adapt their products and services for meeting the demands of a diverse customer base. This approach not only fosters a positive reputation and customer loyalty, but also opens up doors for innovation and expansion. By embracing a more inclusive mindset, companies can position themselves for a long-term success and sustainable growth in the competitive business landscape. For example, a beauty company that caters to different skin tones and hair textures can attract customers who have previously felt marginalized in the industry. By offering products that suits the preferencess of all customers, this company can establish itself as a leader in inclusivity and diversity, ultimately gaining a loyal following and expanding its market reach.

Mahindra is the best example with the Scorpio quickly becoming a hit in the SUV market. Not many people are interested in Tata Motor's "Tata Nano" as a passenger car, but the "Tata Ace" and other commercial cars built on the same platform are big hits. Also, businesses like Fenty Beauty and SheaMoisture reached untapped markets by making products that work for a lot of different skin and hair types. By putting diversity and inclusion at the top of their list of priorities, these beauty brands were able to connect with customers who value reflection and honesty in the industry.

Along with increase in customer base, it also garnered them a loyal following of consumers who appreciate their commitment to diversity and representation. In a market that is often saturated with products that serves a narrow standard of beauty, these brands have stood out by embracing and celebrating the beauty of all individuals. As a result, they made a significant impact in the beauty industry and set a new standard for inclusivity.

RULE 4: SPREAD THE GOOD WORDS

Spread the Good Word, at its core is a strategy in the business and social change worlds, where communication and outreach are very important. Instead of pleasing everyone, this idea says that companies and groups should focus on talking to and reaching out to the exact people who need help with a problem. This practice fits well with the Indian view, which is shaped by the idea of "Jagrukta," or awareness, which is seen as a crucial step toward making this world a better place. There are different cultures, languages, and traditions in India. Each of these aspects brings a unique perspective and understanding to the concept of Jagrukta. By embracing the diversity of India, companies and groups can tailor their communication strategies to effectively reach different communities. Ultimately, by fostering awareness and understanding among the people who need it most, real change and progress can be achieved in both business and social contexts.

This makes it hard for businesses and organizations to connect with a multiple people. Swachh Bharat Abhiyan, a program started by the Indian government to encourage people to be clean and healthy, is an example of this. The campaign has used a variety of ways to get its message out, including media campaigns, community outreach programs, and social media, to make people more aware about practicing good hygiene and sanitation. By utilizing a multifaceted approach, the Swachh Bharat Abhiyan reached a wide audience and effectively convey its message. The program has not only raised awareness about cleanliness but has also inspired real change in the way people view hygiene and sanitation. By connecting with people at individual-level and engaging with communities at large, the campaign made a significant impact on public health and well-being in India. This demonstrates the power of effective communication and outreach in driving positive change in society.

This has led to big changes in the cleanliness of the whole country. Google and other companies around the world show how to spread the good word. Through search engine and advertising platforms, Google has changed how people share information. This has made it easier for companies and groups to talk to their target audiences and get their message across. For example, Google's advertising tool lets companies ensure that their ads reach the right people by targeting them to specific groups of people. As a result, more people are becoming aware of environmental issues and taking action to reduce waste and pollution. Google's efforts in spreading awareness and facilitating communication were undoubtedly significant in improving the overall cleanliness of the country. By leveraging technology and effective communication strategies, Google and other companies are working towards a more sustainable and environmentally conscious society. This demonstrates the power of using modern tools and platforms to drive a positive change on a global scale. For example, Google's Earth Day campaign in 2020 reached millions of users worldwide via its search engine homepage, raising awareness about climate change and suggesting simple ways individuals can reduce their carbon footprint. This increased searches related to sustainable living practices and inspired many to adopt eco-friendly habits in their daily lives.

Bill and Melinda Gates Foundation at Microsoft did a lot of good deeds to get the word out about their group. People from a number of Indian companies are sent to villages to teach in basic schools as part of their onboarding programs. Because of these efforts, more and more people are aware of how their actions affect the world and are taking steps to live in a more sustainable way. Groups like Bill and Melinda Gates Foundation at Microsoft have not only made people more aware, but they have also inspired people to act. This shows that even small changes in behaviour can have a big effect on the world. Companies play a big part in making the future more sustainable for everyone by teaching and giving people power.

In India, this is called "Corporate Social Responsibility," and many PSUs, such as NMDC, BHEL, and HAL, do many good deeds to get the word out. CSR activities raise the brand's value and make people more likely to believe it. By promoting sustainability and social causes, companies like NMDC, BHEL, and HAL improving the lives of those in need, and also enhancing their own reputation and credibility. Through their Corporate Social Responsibility initiatives, these companies are setting an example for others to follow, showing that businesses can make positive impact on society while also thriving in the market. Ultimately, it is this combination of social responsibility and corporate success that will create a sustainable and equitable future for all. For example, NMDC's initiatives to provide education and healthcare to local communities near their mining operations not only benefit those in need but also builds trust with stakeholders. Similarly, BHEL and HAL's efforts to reduce their carbon footprint and support renewable energy projects showcase their commitment to sustainability and social responsibility, earning them respect and admiration from customers and investors alike.

ITC's Lifebuoy campaign or HUL's project "Shakti" also spreads the good words about them. These companies understand the prominence of giving back to the communities that support them and investing in initiatives that promote social and environmental well-being. By prioritizing these values, they are setting positive examples for other businesses to follow. As consumers become more conscious of the impact of their choices, companies like NMDC, BHEL, HAL, ITC, and HUL are positioning themselves as leaders in creating a better world for future generations. Their actions benefit the society, and also contribute to their long-term success and sustainability.

The ALS Ice Bucket Challenge is another global example. It was a social media effort that went viral and raised millions of dollars for ALS research while bringing attention to the disease. The campaign was successful because it used social media to get the word out and get people to join. This shows the importance of clear communication and reaching out to others in order to make good change. To sum up, the idea of "spreading the good word" shows how significant it is to talk to people and reach out to them in order to make positive change. Businesses and groups can make a real difference and work toward a better future by talking to and reaching out to the ones who need help with a problem. By engaging with communities through various communication channels, organizations can effectively raise awareness and mobilize support for important causes. Ultimately, clear and proactive communication is key to driving positive change and fostering collaboration among diverse stakeholders. This approach can increase understanding, empathy, and ultimately, action towards solving pressing issues. By listening to the needs and concerns of others, organizations can tailor their messaging and initiatives to truly improve the lives of those they aim to help.

By actively seeking feedback and input from the community, organizations can ensure that their efforts are in line with the actual needs and priorities of the people they are trying to serve. This not only builds trust and credibility, but also allows for more impactful and sustainable solutions to be developed. Additionally, by fostering open and transparent communication, organizations can foster a sense of ownership and empowerment among community members, leading to greater buy-in and support for their initiatives. In this way, effective communication becomes not just a tool for raising awareness, but a powerful catalyst for positive change and lasting impact. A detailed counterexample would be if an organization fails to effectively communicate with the community they are trying to serve, resulting in misunderstandings and lack of trust. This can lead to resistance towards the organization's initiatives and ultimately hinder their ability to bring a positive change in the community.

For example, a nonprofit organization that works with low-income families may host community meetings to discuss their programs and services, actively listening to feedback and concerns from residents. By openly communicating and involving the community in decision-making processes, the organization can enhance trust and collaboration, ultimately leading to successful outcomes for all involved. Conversely, if the organization fails to provide clear information or engage with community members effectively, misunderstandings may arise, leading to scepticism and resistance towards their efforts. This lack of communication can ultimately hinder the ability of an organization to effectively serve the community and achieve goals. Therefore, it is vital for organizations to prioritize transparent communication and active community engagement in order to foster positive relationships and create meaningful impact. By valuing the input and perspectives of residents, organizations can ensure that their programs and services truly meet the requirements of the community and make a lasting difference.

Reliance Industries Limited: This is India's largest company by market capitalisation, and also the top CSR spender in the country. The company conducts most of its community outreach programs through Reliance Foundation, the CSR arm of the Reliance Group. The main areas of focus of CSR of Reliance Industries include Rural Transformation, Education, Disaster Response, Health, Sports for Development, and Arts, Culture and Heritage.

Tata Consultancy Services Limited: This is a leading IT services, consulting, and business solutions company, and is owned by Tata Group. The organization's mission is to empower individuals and communities, fostering self-sufficiency through purpose-driven technology, all while upholding principles of fairness, equality, and human rights.

It primarily concentrates its CSR efforts on education, skill development, employment, and entrepreneurship, to reduce the opportunity disparity for individuals and communities.

HDFC Bank Limited: This is a leading private sector bank in India, and also one of the highest CSR spenders in the country. The bank's CSR strategy is based on the principle of 'shared value', which means to create economic value which also creates value for society. The main areas of focus of CSR of HDFC Bank are education, healthcare, financial inclusion, environment, and rural development.

RULE 5: DON'T STAY SELF-EMPLOYED

"Don't remain self-employed" is an effective method to sum up smart planning and making the best use of resources. This idea says that business owners should focus on what they do best and what they're passionate about and assign the remaining work to people who can do it better. Indian culture is shaped by the idea of "Dharma," which means doing your job and responsibilities as well as you can. This idea fits well with that ethos. By delegating tasks to experts in their respective fields, business owners can ensure that every aspect of their business is handled with excellence. In Indian culture, there is a deep respect for the division of labour and the idea that each person has a specific role to fulfil. By following the principle of "don't stay self-employed," business owners can not only maximize their own potential but also make a contribution to the overall success of their business.

In a world abundant with talented individuals aspiring to start their own businesses, India has become a breeding ground for success stories. One standout example is Ratan Tata, who propelled Tata Group to become a global leader through his strategic relationships and acquisitions. Tata possessed a remarkable understanding of his own abilities, enabling him to focus on areas where he could make the greatest impact. Simultaneously, he built a capable team to handle other aspects of the business. By leveraging his influential network and making pivotal acquisitions, Tata expanded Tata Group's reach and influence across diverse industries. His adeptness at delegating tasks and capitalizing on his strengths played a crucial role in steering the company towards global triumph.

Similarly, the compelling Sumanta Mokherjee (SUMO) case study further validates the significant growth and success that effective leadership and strategic decision-making can bring to the business landscape. Mokherjee, akin to Tata, displayed exceptional self-awareness by identifying his strengths and weaknesses. To complement his skill set, he assembled a cohesive team that filled in the gaps. Through astute strategic partnerships and key acquisitions, Mokherjee catapulted his company's growth and expanded its market presence. The Tata SUMO case study serves as a poignant reminder of the crucial role played by self-awareness and empowering employees in achieving sustainable growth and resounding success within the business arena.

These remarkable success stories demonstrate that true leaders understand the importance of understanding their own capabilities and limitations. By acknowledging their strengths and weaknesses, they can build teams and foster a collaborative environment that allows everyone to thrive. Leveraging strategic partnerships, the power of delegation, and a deep understanding of individual skill sets, these entrepreneurs have transformed their businesses into global powerhouses.

India's entrepreneurial landscape brims with potential, and countless individuals are prepared to embark on their own business ventures. However, the key lies in emulating the successful strategies adopted by luminaries like Ratan Tata and Sumanta Mokherjee. Through self-awareness, a relentless drive for excellence, and the wisdom to be surrounded by a talented team, these trailblazers have left an indelible mark on the business world.

In a world brimming with possibilities, seize

the opportunity to identify your strengths, embrace self-awareness, and empower your team. By drawing inspiration from the remarkable triumphs witnessed in India, you too can set your sights on unprecedented growth and success. The path to greatness starts with understanding your capabilities, embracing collaboration, and unleashing the collective power of a passionate team. Let these examples guide your journey towards enduring prosperity and influence.

Apple and other companies around the world show what it means to not be self-employed. Steve Jobs, who helped start Apple, was known for putting efforts into product creation and new ideas while giving his team other tasks to do. Apple made products that people liked and was able to set new standards in the tech business by using this method. By empowering his team and fostering a culture of innovation, Jobs led Apple to become a successful company. The company's ability to consistently deliver groundbreaking products and services is a testament to the potency of effective leadership and employee empowerment. In today's dynamic and competitive business environment, companies like Apple serve as a prime example of how self-awareness and employee empowerment can drive sustainable growth and success.

Elon Musk, the visionary CEO of Tesla and

SpaceX, has become a global icon for his ability to transform groundbreaking ideas into reality. His remarkable achievements can be attributed not only to his own brilliance but also to his remarkable capacity to collaborate and inspire others. Musk epitomizes the concept of leveraging collective talents to achieve monumental goals, and the results speak for themselves: revolutionizing electric cars and leading the path for interplanetary travel. What sets Musk apart is his unwavering focus on what he does best while harnessing the skills and expertise of those around him. He understands that true innovation often emerges from the synergy of diverse talents and perspectives. By fostering an environment of collaboration and teamwork, Musk has propelled his companies to unprecedented heights.

Within Tesla and SpaceX, the virtues of collaboration are not merely emphasized but deeply ingrained in the culture. Rather than imposing rigid hierarchies or suffocating bureaucracy, Musk empowers his employees to be creative, take ownership of their work, and contribute meaningfully to the organization's objectives. This drive for innovation and excellence has given rise to a dynamic workforce that consistently pushes boundaries and embraces change-essential qualities in a growingly competitive and fast-paced market.

Musk's leadership style serves as a valuable lesson for businesses across industries. It highlights the significance of cultivating a collaborative, innovative, and forward-thinking environment. By recognizing and tapping into the potential of each team member, companies can unlock new possibilities and drive sustainable growth.

In an era of quick technological advancements and ever-evolving market dynamics, the ability to adapt, innovate, and collaborate has become paramount. Those aspiring to excel in this landscape must embody the spirit of Elon Musk —invigorating leadership, relentless pursuit of ambitious goals, and a commitment to harness the collective power of their teams.

Now is the time to embrace the Muskian mindset, enabling collaboration, fostering creativity, and propelling your business to new horizons. Join the ranks of industry leaders who understand the game-changing power of teamwork and see your organization soar to unprecedented heights. Don't settle for the ordinary when you can achieve the extraordinary with the power of collaboration. Initiate the journey towards a brighter future-start harnessing the collective genius within your own team today.

To sum up, the idea of not being self-employed shows how important it is to plan ahead and work with others when you're in business. Entrepreneurs can build great, long-lasting businesses that do-good things by figuring out strengths and weaknesses, focusing on what they love and what gives them the most value, and forming teams or partnerships to help them out.

RULE 6: SALES SOLVE ALL PROBLEMS:

In the fast-paced and always-evolving world of business, two important ideas are always changing: competition and innovation. In this situation, the term "Sales Solve All Problems" sums up the main idea behind strategic planning and making good use of resources. This idea tells businesses to focus on their main skills and interests, and assign the remainingS work to people who are better at it. This approach encourages people to use their skills more effectively, and also guarantees that the best people for each job are doing it, increasing the success and effectiveness of the company as a whole. By focusing on sales and allowing experts to handle other aspects of the business, companies can make sure they are maximizing their potential for growth and success. This strategy facilitates a more streamlined and efficient operation, as each individual is focuses on their specific strengths and responsibilities. Ultimately, the concept of "Sales Solve All Problems" underscores the significance of specialization and collaboration to thrive in the competitive business world.

This idea fits very well with the idea of "Jugaad," which has a big impact on Indian business culture. This word comes from the Hindi language and means coming up with creative and quick answers to problems, often when you don't have many options. This attitude of being resourceful and creative in finding solutions to problems is deeply ingrained in the Indian entrepreneurial spirit, making it an integral part of the country's business scene. However, the Jugaad answer is only temporary and can't be used again or in other situations. The way it solves the problem is still appreciated here. This mindset of finding quick and innovative solutions has allowed many Indian businesses to thrive in challenging circumstances. It has also led to the emergence of unique and unconventional business practices that have garnered attention worldwide. While Jugaad may not always provide long-term solutions, its capacity to adapt and overcome obstacles quickly has become a defining characteristic of Indian entrepreneurship. Ultimately, this approach reflects the resilience and adaptability that are hallmarks of Indian business culture.

India is full of people who are good at business and have significant untapped potential. There are many stories of people who have followed this advice and gone on amazing journeys to achieve unmatched success in business. There is one star that stands out among all of these success stories: Ratan Tata, the visionary former head of the prestigious Tata Group. Through his unwavering strategic thinking and masterful orchestration of partnerships and deals, he changed the way business is done around the world and took the Tata Group to new heights of wealth and power. Ratan Tata got to the top of the business world not by accident, but because he was very good at figuring out what his skills and weaknesses were and using them to his advantage. He focused his endless energy on areas where it would produce the most results, which he did by smartly finding those areas. This kept him and the Tata Group moving forward with unwavering determination. Just as important was Tata's smart understanding of how important it was to put together a strong team that could handle all the different aspects of the business with unmatched skill and creativity. Ratan Tata's success is so great not only because he was a brilliant person but also because he always believed in working together. His team was able to do great work in their own areas because he knew how to delegate. Meanwhile, he led the ship to new heights. This combination of innovative leadership and a well-coordinated group effort was the key to the Tata Group's unmatched success, which has captured the attention of businesspeople and entrepreneurs all over the world.

Seeing Ratan Tata's amazing trip makes us think about how we want to start our own businesses.

- Are we really making the most of our unique strengths? Are we spending our efforts on the things that will have the biggest effect?
- And finally, and this may be the most important question, are we putting together a team that will enhance our skills?

Let Ratan Tata's amazing legacy always serve as a lesson that the way to true entrepreneurial success lies not only in understanding our own strengths but also in creating space for people to work together and help each other. We can get past problems and write our names on the pages of business history if we work together. Start your journey to greatness right now. Bring out your secret talents, put together a group of amazing people, and make a way that will forever change the world. By harnessing the unique abilities of each team member and fostering an environment of collaboration and support, we can achieve incredible things. Let us strive to emulate the spirit of innovation and teamwork that has made Ratan Tata so successful. Together, we can overcome any challenge and leave a lasting impact on the business world. So, gather your team, unleash your potential, and embark on this journey towards greatness today. The world is waiting for us to make a difference.

Big tech companies like Google show that you don't have to limit yourself to self-employment on a global level. Google changed the way information is shared and spread with its ground-breaking search engine and cutting-edge ad networks. For companies and groups, this has made it easier to talk to their target audiences and get in touch with them more effectively. For example, Google's advertising tool lets companies make ads that are more relevant to certain groups of people, making sure that their ads reach the right people. This has revolutionized the way businesses market their products and services, allowing for more precise targeting and a better return on investment. In addition, Google's suite of tools and services has empowered individuals and small businesses to reach a audience across the world and compete on a level playing field with larger corporations. The impact of Google's innovations has been far-reaching and continues to shape the way we communicate and do business in the digital age.

Elon Musk, the CEO of Tesla and SpaceX, is another famous person around the world who lives by this concept. Musk has made a name for himself with his big, visionary ideas and his skill at making them come true through strategic relationships and teamwork. Musk has been able to change and disrupt many industries, from electric cars to space travel, by focusing on what he does best and using the knowledge of others. His ability to think creatively and push the limits of what's possible has made him a leader in the tech world. Musk's dedication to coming up with new ideas and solving tough problems has inspired many entrepreneurs and businesses to dream big. By following his example, people and companies can work to make a positive impact on the world.

Finally, the idea of not staying self-employed shows how important strategic planning and working together are for entrepreneurs. Entrepreneurs can build long-lasting businesses that not only do well but also do good things for society by figuring out their own strengths and weaknesses, focusing on things they are most passionate about and where they can provide the most value, and building a team or forming partnerships to make up for their weaknesses. By realizing the importance of collaboration and leveraging the strengths of others, entrepreneurs can create businesses that have a sustainable impact on society. Through strategic planning and a focus on social responsibility, entrepreneurs can sync their business goals with making positive changes in the world. Ultimately, by working together and staying true to their values, entrepreneurs can build successful businesses that leave a lasting legacy of positive change.

Rule 7: Don't Run by Preconceived Notions: The Government of India is One of the Largest VCs for Funding.

It's crucial to keep an open mind and consider all available funding options, including those that the government provides. Through a number of funding programs, the Indian government has shown a strong commitment to backing new businesses and ideas. In the business realm, it's commonly believed that individuals who challenge conventional wisdom and approach problems from unique perspectives become successful. From an Indian point of view, this concept is especially important because of the country's long history of new ideas and business spirit. Indian businesspeople who use government funding programs can not only get money but also get access to useful tools and advice that will help their businesses grow and succeed. Innovation and entrepreneurship can thrive in India thanks to the government's efforts.

This makes it easier for people who want to

start their own businesses to make their ideas come true. Indian startups can really benefit from government help and become successful in the competitive business world if they take advantage of these chances and think innovatively about how to get money. There are many cases of entrepreneurs in India who went against the grain and were successful. This is evident from the story of Byju's, an online learning tool. Many people didn't believe that online education would work in India when Byju Raveendran started the business in 2011. But Byju's kept going, and now it's one of the most prosperous edtech companies in the country, worth more than $16 billion. Byju's story shows that Indian startups can solve problems and do well in the market if they are determined and come up with innovative ideas. More Indian entrepreneurs can be like Byju and start great businesses that make a significant difference in their fields if the government supports them and makes the right policies.

The Indian startup environment has a huge amount of room for growth and success. With well-crafted strategies and adequate support, aspiring entrepreneurs can soar to new heights of success. The success of Ola, the site for calling for rides, is another example. When Ankit Bhati and Bhavish Aggarwal started Ola in 2010, the idea of taxi services that you could book through an app was still pretty new in India. Even though it had to deal with problems like governmental hurdles and competition from bigger companies, Ola continuously innovated by generating fresh ideas and expanding its range of services. Today, it stands as one of India's premier ride-hailing apps, boasting millions of users nationwide. Ola's story of success shows that the Indian startup environment has room for growth and new ideas. Ola was able to get a big share of the very competitive ride-hailing market by focusing on making customers happy, improving technology, and making smart relationships.

A big part of the company's success has been its ability in adapting to market changes and always giving people what they want. Indian people who want to be entrepreneurs can have a lot of success and change the startup scene for the better if they have the right idea and are determined. When doing business on a global scale, companies like Airbnb show how not to follow preconceived ideas.

When Brian Chesky and Joe Gebbia started Airbnb in 2008, a lot of people didn't believe that people would rent out their houses to strangers. But Chesky and Gebbia stuck with their plan because they believed in it. Today, Airbnb is a huge company in the hospitality industry, with millions of ads all over the world. Their success comes from being able to shake up the standard hotel business and offer travellers unique, low-cost places to stay. Airbnb has been able to thrive and grow by focusing on building a sense of community and trust among its users. This is a great example for Indian people who want to start their own business because it shows that with creativity and hard work, even the strangest startup ideas can become huge success.

In terms of giving money to startups, the Indian government emerged as one of the biggest venture investors (VCs). The government runs two programs called Startup India and the Atal Innovation Mission that support and pay people who want to start their own businesses. This has made the country more open to innovative ideas and businesses, which have helped companies grow and succeed. In conclusion, the idea that you shouldn't act on assumptions is very important for business success. Entrepreneurs can get past problems and reach their goals by questioning what everyone else thinks and looking outside the box. The Indian government is a big part of encouraging innovation and business in the country through programs like Startup India. This makes India a great place for both startups and investors.

The Indian government has started a number of programs and plans to encourage people to become entrepreneurs and help new businesses stat off. Here are some of the main schemes:

1. Start-up India: This major project, which began in 2016, aims at creating a strong environment for supporting new ideas and companies in India. It helps qualified startups in many ways, like by not charging taxes, letting them self-certify, and giving them money. The goal of Standup India is to encourage women and people from underrepresented groups to become entrepreneurs by giving them money and other help to start new businesses. The country's economy has grown thanks in part to these programs, which have made it easier for new businesses to succeed. India is set to become a world hub for innovation and entrepreneurship if the government keeps supporting and encouraging people to do their best.

2. Stand-Up India is a program that helps women, people from Scheduled Castes (SC), and people from Scheduled Tribes (ST) become entrepreneurs by giving them loans of up to ₹1 crore to start new businesses. People from disadvantaged groups became self-sufficient and financially independent

with the help of Stand-Up India. People have been able to turn their ideas into great businesses thanks to this scheme, which gives them access to money and help. India is on track to get the most out of its diverse people and promote a culture of innovation and entrepreneurship through Stand-Up India and other government programs.

3. Pradhan Mantri Mudra Yojana (PMMY): This program helps small and micro-enterprises that are not farms or corporations get loans of up to 10 lakh rupees. Its goal is to encourage people to start their own businesses and create jobs. People who could not get traditional loans can now follow their dreams of starting a small business, thanks to the Pradhan Mantri Mudra Yojana (PMMY). This project gives people who want to start their own business the tools they need to succeed by giving loans of up to ₹10 lakh. Indian government programs like PMMY are making it possible for a new generation of self-made business owners to start their own companies. These people will help the country's economy grow and improve.

4. The Atal Innovation Mission (AIM) wants to encourage students and new businesses to become creative and start their own businesses. Atal Tinkering Labs, Atal Incubation Centers, and Atal Community Innovation Centers are

some of the projects that are part of it. People can use the tools and get advice from these programs to make their ideas come to life and turn them into businesses that can make money. The Atal Innovation Mission is working to shape India's future economy and make the country a world leader in technology and entrepreneurship by fostering creativity and promoting the generation of new ideas. The government is building a supportive ecosystem that supports and grows the next generation of innovators and job creators through programs like AIM.

5. Skill India: Skill India isn't just about business, but its goal is to teach over 400 million Indians different skills by 2022. This will help more people create jobs instead of looking for them. Skill India is creating a more diverse and competitive workforce by giving people the skills they need to do well in various fields. This program not only gives people the tools needed for making their own chances, but it also helps the country's economy grow as a whole. When AIM and Skill India work together, India builds a culture of creativity, independence,

and innovation that will continue to drive long-term growth for years to come.

6. National SC-ST Hub: This project was started to help businesses from the SC/ST community and to encourage these groups to be more entrepreneurial and creative. The National SC-ST Hub is an important part of the Skill India program because it makes sure that everyone has the same chances to grow and succeed. By giving entrepreneurs from the SC/ST community help and resources, this program is breaking down barriers and making the business world more open and diverse. With the help of AIM, Skill India, and the National SC-ST Hub, India is really building a workforce that is not only skilled and competitive but also comes from diverse backgrounds. NIDHI stands for the National Initiative for Developing and Harnessing Innovations. It is a broad program that supports innovation and business by giving money to startups and incubators. NIDHI is very important for encouraging innovation and entrepreneurship in India because it gives startups money and other

resources to help them achieve. NIDHI helps in building a strong environment for innovation and economic growth by giving money to new businesses and the groups that help them grow. When programs like NIDHI are in place, India is ready to keep moving toward its goal of becoming a world centre for innovation and startups.

7. The Prime Minister Employment Generation Programme (PMEGP) is another government program that helps small businesses in both cities and rural areas by giving them money. Its goal is to encourage people to become entrepreneurs. Through the PMEGP, people who want to start their own businesses can get loans and other financial help to do so. This helps create jobs and boosts the economy. Together, programs like NIDHI and PMEGP give people the tools they require to follow their business dreams and help India's startup community grow.

The Ministry of MSME works on all of the above big projects with other ministries, departments, and boards. There are different ideas for each of them to get people in India to start their own businesses. The Ministry of Science and Technology helps the electronics business, for instance. People are told to follow their dreams by the Department of Science and Technology (DST). The Department of Animal Husbandry in the Central Government also helps companies that work on dairy development in the same way. Fishing projects get help from the National Fisheries Development Boards, and honey companies get help from the National Board of Honeybees in the Ministry of Agriculture. The Ministry of Micro, Small, and Medium Enterprises (MSME) also has a number of programs and rewards to encourage people to start their own businesses and help these areas grow. Startup India helps aspiring business owners all over the country by giving them money, advice, and chances to meet other people in the same field. These government programs not only help businesses that are already up and running, but they also support new businesses to start up and grow, which is good for the economy. The government of India wants to make it easier for businesses to grow and new ideas to come up by giving companies in different fields help and resources. Along with other programs, these are very important for making India an entrepreneurial place and helping new and small businesses grow all over the coutry.

CHAPTER 3: MINDSET

Let's delve into the essential chapters of our entrepreneurial journey, akin to a well-crafted manuscript. As we embark on this entrepreneurial leadership voyage where we train our mind to act more responsible. Responsibilities give the maturity and maturity gives the wisdom. With each challenge we face and overcome, we gain invaluable insights and experiences that shape us into better leaders. Just as a manuscript is refined through editing and revision, our entrepreneurial journey is honed through learning from our mistakes and adapting to new circumstances. As we continue to embrace our responsibilities and grow in maturity, we will ultimately become wise and successful entrepreneurs.

In the following chapters we'll explore the intricacies that define the path of hustlers and entrepreneurs. Each chapter unfolds like a page-turner, revealing wisdom and insights that resonate with the spirit of leadership.

Chapter A: Self-Reflection – The Prologue

In this opening chapter, we pause to gaze inward. Self-reflection becomes our ink, and introspection our quill. We delve into our motivations, fears, and aspirations. What drives us? What are our strengths and weaknesses? As the dawn breaks, we pen our own narrative, understanding that self-awareness is the cornerstone of success.

Chapter B: Assessing Skills and Knowledge – The Foundation

Our protagonist, the budding entrepreneur, sharpens their tools. They assess their skills, honing their craft. Knowledge becomes their compass, guiding them through uncharted waters. We explore the art of continuous learning – the alchemy that transforms raw potential into expertise.

Chapter C: Seeking Feedback – The Critical Review

Entrepreneurs, like seasoned authors, seek feedback. They invite constructive criticism, knowing that growth lies in the margins. We learn to embrace feedback as a gift, refining our chapters until they gleam. The best leaders recognize that vulnerability is their greatest strength.

Chapter D: Setting Goals – The Plot Arc

Our narrative gains structure as we set ambitious goals. Like plot twists, these objectives propel us forward. We visualize the climax – the summit we aspire to reach. Goals become our guiding stars, illuminating the path ahead.

Chapter E: Identifying Values – The Moral Compass

Entrepreneurs, like characters in an epic saga, adhere to their core values. Integrity, empathy, and authenticity form the spine of their tale. We explore the ethical dilemmas faced by leaders, knowing that values shape destinies.

Chapter F: Assessing the Situation – The Turning Point

The entrepreneur stands at the crossroads. They analyze market trends, assess risks, and weigh opportunities. The situation becomes their canvas, and strategic decisions their brushstrokes. We unravel the art of calculated risk-taking.

Chapter G: Learning Opportunities – The Subplots

Entrepreneurs are voracious readers, devouring knowledge from diverse sources. We explore the hidden gems – workshops, mentors, and serendipitous encounters. Learning becomes our subplot, enriching the main narrative.

Chapter H: Tracking Progress – The Word Count

Numbers tell our story. Metrics become our chapters – revenue, growth, and customer satisfaction. We learn to measure progress objectively, adjusting our plotlines as needed. Persistence fuels our inkwell.

Chapter I: Challenging Yourself – The Climax

The hero faces their greatest adversary – themselves. Entrepreneurs embrace discomfort, scaling peaks that seemed insurmountable. We delve into resilience, knowing that adversity births character.

Chapter J: Patience and Persistence – The Epilogue

Our tale nears its end. Patience, the quiet companion, whispers, "Trust the process." Persistence, the unwavering scribe, etches the final lines. We bid farewell, knowing that every chapter shapes our legacy.

And yes, in the ancient verses of the **Ramayana**, we find echoes of these very qualities – in Rama's unwavering commitment, Sita's resilience, and Hanuman's tireless pursuit. The epic itself is a testament to leadership – a timeless manuscript passed down through generations. If you are eager to know further may be you should go for another book written by me "Be the Leader, Not A Boss!" You will find the book in Amazon.

So, fellow Hustlers of destiny, let us write our chapters with ink forged from determination, courage, and vision. Our story awaits its readers – the world.

ATTRIBUTE A: SELF-REFLECTION

Take a moment to reflect on your experiences, achievements, and challenges. Consider what you excel at, what brings you joy, and where you face difficulties. Reflecting on past successes and failures can offer valuable insights into your capabilities. This self-assessment can assist in identifying areas for growth and improvement, while also reinforcing your strengths. It is important to be honest with yourself during this process, acknowledging both your successes and areas where you need to make changes. By taking the time to reflect over your experiences, achievements, and challenges, you can better understand yourself and make informed decisions about your future goals and aspirations.

In the fast-paced world we live in, it's easy to become engrossed in the hustle and bustle of daily existence, forgetting to pause and reflect on our journey. However, self-reflection is a crucial tool for personal and professional growth. From an Indian perspective, this practice is deeply ingrained in our culture, with concepts like "Atma-Gyan" (self-awareness) and "Swarajya" (self-rule) emphasizing the significance of knowing oneself. By taking the time to reflect on our experiences, achievements, and challenges, we can analyze our strengths and weaknesses. This self-awareness empowers us to establish realistic goals and make informed decisions about our future. In a world characterized by constant change and evolution, the capacity to adapt and evolve is indispensable. By practicing self-reflection, we can ensure that we are continuously learning and improving, both personally and professionally. It is through this process that we can truly achieve self-rule and lead a fulfilling and purposeful life.

In India, there are multiple examples of individuals who have embraced the practice of self-reflection and achieved great success. One such example is Mahatma Gandhi, who famously said, "The best way to find yourself is to lose yourself in the service of others." Gandhi's life was a testament to the power of self-reflection, as he constantly examined his beliefs and actions to align them with his values. His commitment to nonviolent resistance and and his selfless dedication to serving others serve as an inspiring model for individuals worldwide. By emulating Gandhi's principles and emphasizing self-reflection, we too can endeavor to leave a positive imprint on our communities and society at large. It is through this introspective journey that we can unearth our true purpose and effect meaningful change in the world.

Another example is the Indian cricket team under the leadership of Virat Kohli. Kohli is known for his intense self-reflection and his ability to learn from his mistakes. This approach has not only made him a great cricketer of all time but also a role model for aspiring athletes around the world. By following Kohli's example of commitment to self-reflection, athletes can aspire to enhance their skills and positively influence their teams. Through introspection and a willingness to learn and grow, individuals like Kohli and Gandhi show us that personal development is not only important for individual success but also for the betterment of society as a whole. It is through this commitment to self-improvement and effecting positive change in the world that we can truly leave a lasting legacy.

Companies like Google are excellent examples of the value of self-reflection on a global scale. Google encourages its employees to take time for self-reflection through initiatives like "20% time," where employees can allocate a part of their workweek to projects of their preference. This practice has led to some of Google's most innovative products, such as Gmail and Google Maps. These innovations not only boost Google's success in the competitive tech industry but also have a positive impact on society by improving communication and navigation for people worldwide. By prioritizing self-reflection and personal growth, Google has set a standard for other companies to follow, demonstrating that focusing on individual development can lead to groundbreaking advancements that benefit overall society. In this way, the commitment to self-improvement not only leaves a lasting legacy for the individual but also creates a ripple effect that can shape the future for generations to come.

In conclusion, self-reflection serves as a powerful tool for both personal and professional advancement. Through deliberate contemplation of our experiences, achievements, and challenges, we attain valuable insights into our abilities, thereby enabling us to navigate a path towards success.

Here is one approach:

What is self-reflection and why is it important? Self-reflection is the process of examining one's own thoughts, feelings, actions, and outcomes in relation to one's goals, values, and aspirations. It is a vital skill for anyone aspiring to enhance themselves and realize their full potential.

Self-reflection can help us in many ways. For

instance, it can help us:

- Identify our strengths and weaknesses, and work on them accordingly.

- Recognize our passions and interests and pursue them with enthusiasm.

- Learn from our successes and failures and use them as opportunities for growth.

- Develop a sense of purpose and direction and align our actions with our vision.

- Enhance our self-awareness and self-confidence and appreciate our uniqueness.

- Foster a positive mindset and attitude and overcome challenges with resilience.

- Build meaningful relationships and connections, and actively contribute to the well-being of others.

Self-reflection is not a one-time activity, but a continuous practice that requires time, effort, and commitment. It is not always easy or comfortable, but it is always rewarding and empowering.

How to practice self-reflection? There is no one right way to practice self-reflection, as different methods may suit different people and situations. However, some general guidelines that can help are:

- Allocate a dedicated time and space for self-reflection, preferably in a quiet and distraction-free environment.

- Use a journal, a notebook, or a digital device to

record your thoughts and insights, as writing can help you organize and articulate your ideas.

- Ask yourself open-ended and probing questions that challenge you to think deeply and critically about yourself and your experiences. Some examples of such questions are:

- What are my goals and how am I progressing towards them?

- What are my values and how do they guide my decisions and actions?

- What are my achievements and what are the contributing factors?

- What are my challenges and what are the lessons that I learned from them?

- What are my skills and talents and how can I use them to benefit myself and others?

- What are my passions and hobbies and how do they enrich my life?

- What areas do I need to improve upon and how can I work on them?

- How do I cope with stress and adversity and how can I improve my coping strategies?

- How do I interact with others and how can I improve my communication and collaboration skills?

- How do I balance my personal and professional life and how can I achieve a healthy harmony?

- Be honest and objective with yourself and avoid being too harsh or too lenient. Acknowledge both your positive and negative aspects and celebrate your achievements as well as acknowledge your mistakes.

- Be open-minded and curious and seek feedback and perspectives from others who can offer you constructive criticism and support. Listen to their opinions and suggestions, but also trust your own judgment and intuition.

- Be flexible and adaptable and embrace change and uncertainty as inevitable and essential parts of life. Be willing to experimenting with new ideas and approaches and learn from your outcomes and experiences.

- Be consistent and persistent and make self-reflection a regular habit that you incorporate into your daily or weekly routine. Review your progress and results periodically, and adjust your goals and strategies as needed.

Self-reflection serves a powerful tool for both personal and professional development. By dedicating time to reflect on our experiences, achievements, and challenges, we gain valuable insights into our capabilities and chart a course for success. As the famous philosopher Socrates said, "The unexamined life is not worth living." Therefore, be your own best friend and talk with him the most internally. You may discover patterns in your behaviour or thought processes that are holding you back, and by recognizing these patterns, you can work towards making positive changes. Embrace the journey of self-discovery and be open to learning more about yourself. With self-reflection as a consistent practice, you will not only grow personally and professionally, but you will also develop a deeper sense of self-awareness and fulfilment. Remember, the more you invest in yourself, the more you will reap the benefits in all aspects of your life.

ATTRIBUTE B: ASSESS SKILLS AND KNOWLEDGE

Make a list of your skills, competencies, and areas of expertise. Consider both hard skills (technical skills) and soft skills (communication, leadership, problem-solving, etc.). Evaluate how proficient you are in each skill and identify areas to improve.

In the intricate tapestry of personal and professional development, the deliberate examination of one's skills and knowledge stand as a cornerstone. Within the rich cultural backdrop of India, this introspective practice resonates deeply with the profound notion of "Svadhyaya." Translated as the dedicated pursuit of self-study and self-analysis, Svadhyaya embodies a fundamental principle crucial for fostering self-enhancement and advancement on both personal and professional fronts. Rooted in ancient wisdom, the sacred concept of Svadhyaya beckons individuals to begin a transformative journey of self-discovery and improvement. By peering inward and reflecting on one's abilities, limitations, and aspirations, one can illuminate pathways to growth and actualization. This introspective process acts as a guiding beacon, offering insights into areas ripe for development and refinement.

Embracing Svadhyaya empowers individuals to craft a roadmap for their own evolution, steering them towards a more fulfilling and purposeful existence. Through the lens of self-assessment, one gains a profound understanding of their unique strengths and weaknesses, facilitating targeted growth and progress. In the tapestry of personal and professional development, Svadhyaya emerges as a timeless practice nurturing self-awareness and fostering a culture of continuous learning and improvement.

Just as a sculptor chisel away at rough stone to reveal a masterpiece within, Svadhyaya invites individuals to start a transformative journey of self-refinement and discovery. By embracing this profound practice of self-study and introspection, one can unlock hidden potentials, transcend limitations, and sculpt a future imbued with growth and self-actualization.

In India, there are multiple examples of individuals who have excelled in their fields by diligently assessing their skills and knowledge. One such example is Sundar Pichai, the CEO of Google. Pichai started his career as a software engineer and rose through the ranks by continuously upgrading his technical skills while also honing his soft skills, such as communication and leadership. His ability to assess his skills and identify areas to improve has played a key role in his success.

Another example is the Indian cricket team captain, Mithali Raj. Raj is known for her impeccable batting skills, but she has also worked on improving her leadership and communication skills, which are essential for leading a team. Her commitment to assessing her skills and knowledge has made her one of the most successful cricketers in the world.

On a global scale, companies like Amazon exemplify the importance of assessing skills and knowledge. Amazon has a culture of continuous learning and encourages its employees to regularly assess their skills and identify the areas for improvement. This practice has helped Amazon in staying ahead of the curve in a rapidly evolving tech landscape.

In conclusion, assessing skills and knowledge is necessary for personal and professional development. By actively assessing our skills, competencies, and areas of expertise, we can pinpoint areas for improvement and take proactive measures to enhance our capabilities.

Assessing Skills and Knowledge: How to Evaluate and Improve Your Capabilities

What are skills and knowledge, and why are they important? Skills and knowledge are the abilities and information that we acquire through education, training, experience, and practice. They are essential for performing various tasks and activities in our personal and professional lives.

Skills and knowledge can be classified into two broad categories: hard skills and soft skills. Hard skills are technical skills that are specific to a particular domain or field, such as programming, accounting, or engineering. Soft skills are interpersonal skills that are applicable across various domains and fields, such as communication, leadership, problem-solving, or teamwork.

Both hard skills and soft skills are important for achieving success and satisfaction in our careers and lives. Hard skills enable us to perform our tasks efficiently and effectively, while soft skills enable us to interact with others harmoniously and collaboratively. Together, they form a comprehensive set of capabilities that can help us achieve our goals and aspirations.

How do you assess skills and knowledge?

Assessing skills and knowledge involves

measuring and evaluating how proficient we are in each skill and area of knowledge. It is a vital step for identifying our strengths and weaknesses and finding areas where we can improve.

There are various methods and tools that can help us assess our skills and knowledge, such as:

Self-assessment: This is the process of reflecting on our own skills and knowledge and rating ourselves on a scale of 1 to 10, where 1 is the lowest and 10 is the highest. We can use a simple checklist or a more detailed questionnaire to guide our self-assessment. The advantages of self-assessment are that it is easy, convenient, and inexpensive. The disadvantages are that it can be subjective, biased, or inaccurate.

Feedback: This is the process of seeking opinions and suggestions from others who have observed or interacted with us, such as our managers, colleagues, clients, or mentors. We can use formal or informal methods to gather feedback, like surveys, interviews, or conversations. The advantages of feedback are that it is objective, reliable, and constructive. The disadvantages are that it can be difficult, time-consuming, or costly.

Tests: This is the process of taking standardized or customized tests that measure our skills and knowledge, such as aptitude tests, skill tests, or knowledge tests. We can use online or offline platforms to access and complete the tests. The advantages of tests are that they are valid, consistent, and comparable. The disadvantages are that they can be stressful, challenging, or limited.

How do you improve skills and knowledge? Improving skills and knowledge is a process of enhancing and expanding our abilities and information through learning and practice. It is a continuous and lifelong process that requires time, effort, and commitment.

There are various sources and resources that can help us improve our skills and knowledge, such as:

Education: This is the process of acquiring formal or informal education that provides us with theoretical and practical knowledge, such as degrees, diplomas, certificates, or courses. We can use online or offline platforms to access and enrol in various educational programs. The advantages of education are that it is comprehensive, structured, and recognized. The disadvantages are that it can be expensive, lengthy, or rigid.

Training: This is the process of receiving specific or general training that provides us with hands-on and experiential learning, such as workshops, seminars, webinars, or coaching. We can use online or offline platforms to access and participate in various training programs. The advantages of training are that it is interactive, engaging, and relevant. The disadvantages are that it can be scarce, variable, or outdated.

Experience: This is the process of gaining direct or indirect experience that provides us with practical and contextual learning, such as projects, assignments, tasks, or volunteering. We can use online or offline platforms to access and pursue various opportunities for experience. The advantages of experience are that it is authentic, meaningful, and rewarding. The disadvantages are that it can be risky, challenging, or unpredictable.

Assessing skills and knowledge is an important step towards personal and professional growth. By making a list of our skills, competencies, and areas of expertise and evaluating how proficient we are in each of them, we can identify areas where we can improve and take proactive measures to enhance our capabilities. As the famous author and speaker Brian Tracy said, "The more you learn, the more you earn."

ATTRIBUTE C: SEEK FEEDBACK

Ask friends, coworkers, mentors, or supervisors you trust for feedback. From the outside, they can give you useful information about your strengths and weaknesses. Be willing to hear constructive criticism and use it to figure out where you need to improve. Feedback is important for personal as well as professional growth. It helps us see ourselves more clearly and figure out how other people see us. When we ask people we trust for feedback, we can see things from a different angle and learn how to get better. Accepting helpful feedback is essential to get better and reach our goals.

In the pursuit of personal and professional development, seeking feedback from others is a key practice that can offer valuable insights and perspectives. From an Indian viewpoint, this aligns with the concept of "Guru-Shishya Parampara," which underscores the importance of learning from mentors and guides to enhance one's knowledge and skills. By incorporating feedback and guidance from trusted individuals, we can identify areas for growth and make meaningful changes to become the best version of ourselves. This approach fosters personal development, strengthens relationships, and cultivates an environment of continuous learning and improvement. In essence, embracing feedback as a tool for self-improvement is a powerful way to navigate life's challenges and achieve our aspirations.

In India, there are many such examples of individuals who have benefited from seeking feedback. One such example is Dr. APJ Abdul Kalam, the former President of India. Dr. Kalam was known for his humility and openness to feedback, which allowed him to constantly learn and grow. He sought feedback from colleagues, students, and experts in various fields, which helped him become a respected scientist and leader.

Another example is the Indian cricket team captain, Virat Kohli. Kohli is known for his aggressive and dynamic leadership style, but he also realizes the importance of feedback. He regularly seeks feedback from his teammates, coaches, and mentors, which has helped him improve his game and become one of the best cricketers in the world. By being open to feedback, Kohli could adapt and evolve his approach to leadership, making him not only a successful captain but also a role model for younger players. His willingness to listen and learn from others has played a significant role in his success on and off the field. Like Dr. Kalam, Virat Kohli's ability to seek feedback and constantly strive for improvement has made him a respected figure in his field.

On a global scale, companies like Microsoft exemplify the importance of seeking feedback. Microsoft has a culture of feedback, where employees are encouraged to provide and receive feedback from their peers and supervisors. This approach has enabled Microsoft to nurture a culture of continual improvement and innovation. Their dedication to soliciting feedback has kept them at the forefront of the competition, allowing them to respond effectively to shifting market dynamics. By attentively listening to both customers and employees, Microsoft has been able to innovate new products and services tailored to their target demographic. In an ever-changing landscape, the capacity to seek feedback and pivot accordingly is paramount for sustained success, and Microsoft's exemplar underscores the significance of this approach.

In conclusion, seeking feedback is essential for personal and professional growth. By actively seeking feedback from trusted individuals, we gain valuable insights into our strengths and weaknesses and identify areas for improvement. Being open to constructive criticism and utilizing it to enhance our skills and capabilities can help us achieve greater success in our endeavors.

Seeking Feedback: How to Learn and Grow from Others' Perspectives

What is feedback, and why is it important? Feedback is the information and opinions that we receive from others regarding our performance, behaviour, or outcomes. It is an important source of learning and growth, as helps us:

Understand how others perceive us and our work and how we can improve our impression and impact.

Recognize our strengths and weaknesses and how we can leverage our strengths and address our weaknesses.

Discover new opportunities and challenges and how we can pursue them or overcome them.

Validate our assumptions and expectations and how we can align them with reality.

Motivate and inspire us, and how we can sustain our enthusiasm and passion.

Feedback can vary in nature, ranging from positive to negative, formal to informal, solicited to unsolicited and specific to general, contingent upon the context and intended purpose. However, regardless of the type of feedback, it is crucial to be open and receptive to it and use it as a catalyst for our growth.

How do I seek feedback? Seeking feedback includes actively asking for and obtaining feedback from others who can provide us with valuable insights and perspectives. It is a key practice for individuals who want to improve themselves and achieve their full potential.

Seeking feedback can be done in various ways, such as:

Asking for feedback from trusted friends, colleagues, mentors, or supervisors who can provide us with honest and constructive feedback. We can use a simple or detailed feedback form to guide the feedback process, or we can use a casual or formal conversation to elicit the feedback. We can also specify the areas or aspects that we want feedback on, or we can ask for general feedback.

Seeking feedback from multiple sources and perspectives that can provide us with diverse and comprehensive feedback. We can seek feedback from people who have different roles, backgrounds, experiences, or opinions and who can offer us different insights and suggestions. We can also seek feedback from people who have different levels of expertise, authority, or influence and who can offer us different levels of feedback.

Seeking feedback regularly and consistently from someone who can provide us with timely and relevant feedback. We can seek feedback at various stages of our projects, tasks, or activities, such as before, during, or after completion. We can seek feedback at different intervals in our career or life, such as monthly, quarterly, or annually.

How do I use feedback? Using feedback is the process of analyzing and applying the feedback that we receive from others to enhance our skills and capabilities. It is a crucial step for turning feedback into action and results.

Using feedback can be done in various ways, such as:

Reviewing and reflecting on the feedback and identifying the key themes, patterns, and messages. We can use a feedback summary or a feedback report to organize and present the feedback, or we can use a feedback matrix or a feedback map to visualize and categorize the feedback. We can also compare and analyze the feedback gathered from various sources and perspectives and look for similarities and differences, evaluating and prioritizing the feedback and deciding which feedback to act on and which feedback to ignore.

We can use a feedback criterion or a feedback scorecard to assess and rank the feedback, or we can use a feedback matrix or a feedback map to prioritize and classify the feedback. We can also consider the validity, reliability, and relevance of the feedback and look for evidences and examples. By carefully analyzing the feedback using these tools, we gain valuable insights into the areas that require improvement or further development. Additionally, by considering the validity, reliability, and relevance of the feedback, we can ensure that our actions are based on accurate and meaningful information. Incorporating feedback analysis into our decision-making process helps us make more informed choices and ultimately enhance our performance and outcomes.

Implementing and monitoring the feedback and taking concrete steps to improve our performance, behaviour, or outcomes. We can use a feedback action plan or a feedback roadmap to outline and execute the feedback, or we can use a feedback tracker or a feedback dashboard to measure and track the feedback. We can also seek feedback on our feedback implementation and monitoring and look for progress and improvement.

Seeking feedback is crucial for both personal and professional growth. By asking for and obtaining feedback from trusted individuals, we get valuable insights and perspectives into our strengths and weaknesses to identify areas for our improvement. By being open to constructive criticism and using it to enhance our skills and capabilities, we can achieve greater success in our endeavors. Additionally, seeking feedback builds stronger relationships with our colleagues and peers, as it shows that we value their opinions and are committed to continuous improvement. By actively seeking feedback, we exhibit our readiness to learn and evolve, fostering greater trust and respect from those in our circle. Ultimately, incorporating feedback into our personal and professional development leads to a more fulfilling and successful career.

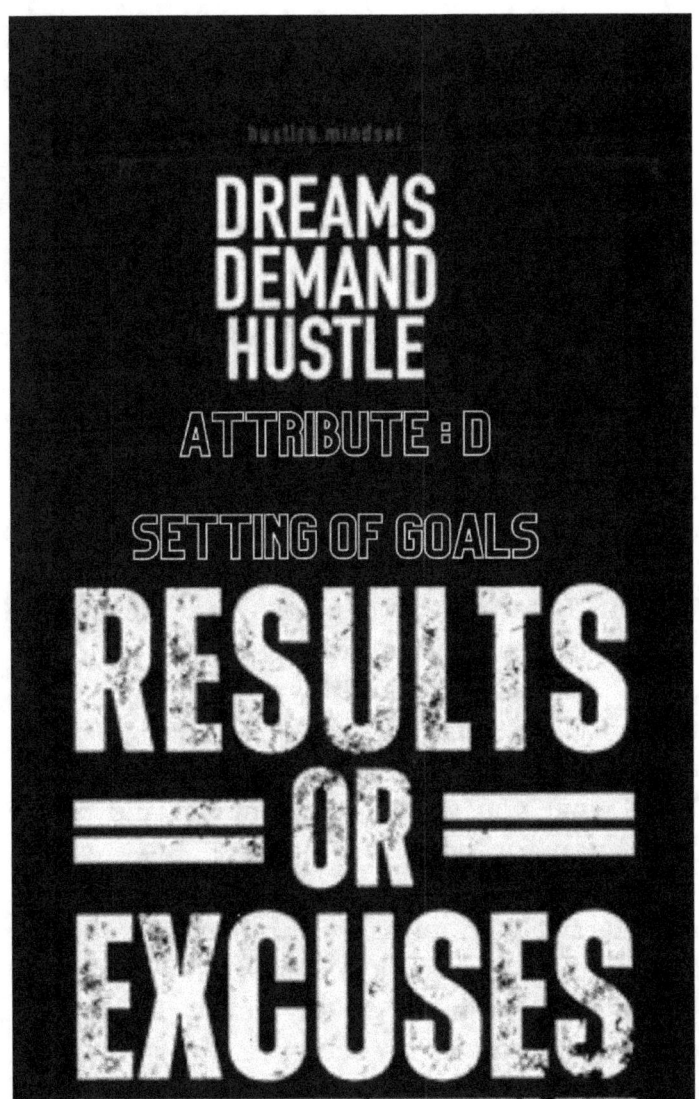

ATTRIBUTE D: SETTING OF GOALS

Always set Specific, Measurable, Achievable, Relevant, and Time-Bound (SMART) Goals for Yourself. Determine What You Want to Achieve and What Capabilities You Need to Develop to Reach Your Goals. Break Down Larger Goals into Smaller Milestones to Track Your Progress. By setting SMART goals, you are able to clearly define what you want to accomplish and create a roadmap for how to get there. By breaking down larger goals into smaller milestones, you can effectively monitor your progress and stay motivated as you work towards achieving your objectives. Remember to regularly review and adjust your goals as needed to ensure you are on track to reaching your desired outcomes.

In the pursuit of personal and professional growth, setting goals is a fundamental practice that provides direction and motivation. From an

Indian perspective, this principle resonates with the concept of "Sankalpa," which refers to a strong determination to achieve a specific goal or purpose. By incorporating the idea of Sankalpa into your goal-setting process, you can infuse your objectives with a profound sense of purpose and dedication. This cultural perspective highlights the importance of perseverance and commitment in achieving success. By staying true to your Sankalpa and regularly reassessing your goals, you can cultivate a mindset of continuous growth and improvement.

In India, there are numerous examples of individuals who have achieved great success by setting and pursuing their goals. One such example is Raghuram Rajan, the former Governor of the Reserve Bank of India. Rajan set a goal early in his career to make significant contributions to the fields of economics and finance. Through hard work, dedication, and strategic goal-setting, he achieved this goal and became a respected economist in the world.

Another example is the Indian space agency, ISRO (Indian Space Research Organisation). ISRO has set ambitious goals for itself, such as launching satellites into space and exploring Mars. By establishing specific, measurable, achievable, relevant, and time-bound (SMART) goals, ISRO has achieved remarkable advancements in space technology, solidifying its position as a global leader in space exploration. Among ISRO's notable achievements is the successful launch of a record-breaking 104 satellites in a single mission, demonstrating their innovation and efficiency in space technology. By consistently setting and achieving ambitious goals, ISRO has paved the way for India to become a significant player in the global space industry and has inspired other countries to collaborate and learn from their success. The agency's commitment to excellence and strategic goal-setting has solidified its reputation as a powerhouse in space exploration and a leader in pushing the limits of what is achievable in outer space.

On a global scale, companies like Google exemplify the importance of setting goals. Google sets ambitious goals for its products and services, such as organizing the world's information and making it accessible and useful universally. By setting clear and measurable goals, Google has pioneered innovation and developed products that have revolutionized how we access information.

In conclusion, setting goals is essential for personal and professional growth. By setting SMART goals and breaking them into smaller milestones, we can track our progress and stay motivated. Whether it's achieving success in our careers or making a transformative impact in society, setting goals can help us turn our dreams into reality.

Setting Goals: A Guide to Achieving Your Dreams and Aspirations

What are goals and why are they important? Goals are the desired outcomes or results that we want to achieve in our personal or professional lives. They are important because they:

- Provide us with a clear and specific direction and focus and help us avoid distractions and procrastination.
- Inspire and motivate us to act and overcome challenges and help us maintain our enthusiasm and passion.
- Measure and evaluate our performance and progress and help us identify our strengths and weaknesses.
- Reward and celebrate our achievements and successes and help us appreciate our efforts and accomplishments.

Goals can be short-term or long-term, depending on the time frame and scope. However, irrespective of the type of goals, they should be SMART, which stands for:

- **Specific:** Goals should be clear and precise, and

state exactly what we want to achieve and why. For example, instead of saying "I want to learn a new skill," we can say "I want to learn how to play the guitar because I love music and want to express myself creatively."

- **Measurable:** Goals should be quantifiable and verifiable, and state how we will measure and track our progress and results. For instance, instead of saying "I want to improve my health," we can say "I want to lose 10 kg of weight and lower my blood pressure by 10 points in six months."

- **Achievable:** Goals should be realistic and attainable, and state how we will achieve them and what resources we need. For example, instead of saying "I want to become a millionaire," we can say "I want to increase my income by 20% in one year by working hard, saving more, and investing wisely."

- **Relevant:** Goals should be meaningful and aligned with our values and aspirations, and state how they will benefit us and others. For example, instead of saying "I want to travel the world," we can say "I want to visit 10 countries in five years to learn about different cultures and make new friends.

- **Time-bound:** Goals should have a specific deadline or time frame, and state when we will start and finish them. For example, instead of saying "I want to write a book," we can say "I want to write a 300-page novel in three months, starting from January 1st and ending on March 31st."

How to set goals? Setting goals is the process of defining and planning our desired outcomes or results. It is a key practice for anyone committed to improve themselves and achieve their full potential.

Setting goals can be done in various steps, such as:

- Brainstorming and listing our dreams and aspirations and identifying what we want to achieve in our personal or professional lives. We can use a mind map, a vision board, or a bucket list to visualize and organize our ideas.

- Prioritizing and selecting our most important and urgent goals and deciding which ones to focus on and pursue. We can use a priority matrix, a Pareto chart, or a SWOT analysis to evaluate and rank our goals.

- Refining and formulating our goals using the SMART criteria, and making them clear, measurable, achievable, relevant, and time-bound. We can use a goal statement, a goal worksheet, or a goal contract to write and document our goals.

- Breaking down and dividing our larger goals into smaller and manageable milestones and defining the steps and actions to be taken to achieve them. We can use a goal ladder, a Gantt chart, or a timeline to plan and schedule our goals.

- Reviewing and revising our goals periodically and checking our progress and results. We can use a goal tracker, a progress report, or a feedback loop to monitor and measure our goals.

Setting goals is essential for personal and professional growth. By setting SMART goals and breaking them into smaller milestones, we can track our progress and stay motivated. Whether it's achieving success in our careers or bringing a positive change in society, setting goals can help us turn our dreams into reality. By utilizing tools such as a goal ladder, Gantt chart, or timeline, we can effectively plan and schedule our goals to ensure we are on track. Additionally, regularly reviewing and revising our goals, as well as monitoring our progress with a goal tracker or progress report, allows us to make the necessary adjustments and remain focused on our objectives. Ultimately, setting and actively working towards our goals enables us to not only achieve personal and professional growth, but also turn our aspirations into tangible achievements.

It is essential to remember that setting goals is an ongoing process that requires dedication and perseverance. By breaking down our goals into smaller, manageable tasks and celebrating our achievements along the way, we can stay motivated and inspired to continue moving forward. With a clear vision and a strategic plan in place, we can overcome challenges and setbacks, ultimately realizing our full potential. In the end, the journey toward achieving our goals is as significant as the destination itself, as it teaches valuable lessons and molds us into the finest versions of ourselves.

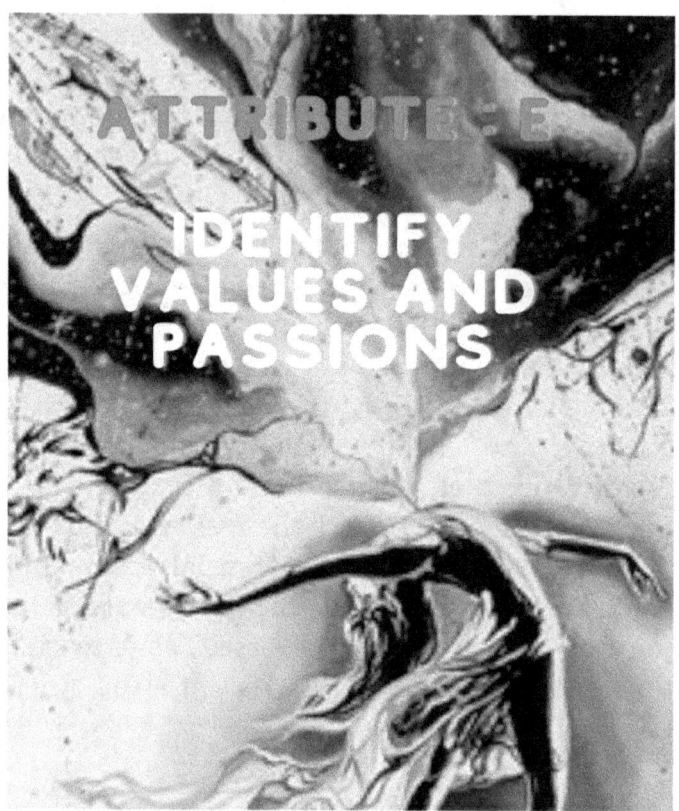

DONT LOSE YOUR FIRE.

ATTRIBUTE E: IDENTIFY VALUES AND PASSIONS

Think about your beliefs, hobbies, and deepest desires. How do you get motivated? What do you like to do? Aligning your skills with your values and interests can help you be happier and more successful in what you're doing. When you are passionate about your pursuits, maintaining motivation and focus becomes more effortless. By pinpointing your values and passions, you can cultivate a sense of purpose and fulfilment in your endeavors. This alignment can lead to increased productivity, satisfaction, and overall success in both your personal and professional lives.

In the journey of personal and professional growth, understanding one's values and passions is crucial for finding fulfilment and success. From an Indian perspective, this principle resonates deeply with the concept of "Dharma," which emphasizes living a life in alignment with one's values and purpose. By incorporating the idea of Dharma into your daily life, you can make sure that your actions are in line with your true self, leading to a sense of harmony and contentment. This ancient philosophy encourages individuals to follow their passions and values, ultimately leading to a more fulfilling and purposeful existence. By embracing this concept, you can overcome the challenges of life with clarity and confidence, ultimately achieving success and happiness in all aspects of your life.

In India, there are many individuals who have found success by aligning their capabilities with their values and passions. One such example is Dr. APJ Abdul Kalam, the former President of India. Dr. Kalam was passionate about science and technology, and he dedicated his life to advancing India's space and missile programs. His alignment with his values and passions not only led to a successful career but also earned him respect and admiration worldwide. Dr. Kalam's clarity of purpose and unwavering dedication to his work allowed him to overcome obstacles and achieve great heights in his career. His ability to stay true to his values and passions served as a guiding light, inspiring others to follow the same. By following his example, individuals can harness their own strengths and passions to navigate life's challenges confidently and purposefully, ultimately finding success and fulfilment in their endeavors.

Another example is Mother Teresa, who devoted her life to serving the poor, needy and destitute in Kolkata. Despite encountering numerous challenges, Mother Teresa remained unwavering in her dedication to helping others, showcasing the potency of aligning one's abilities with one's values and passions.

On a global scale, individuals like Elon Musk exemplify the importance of aligning values and passions with capabilities. Musk is passionate about space exploration and renewable energy, and he has built successful companies like SpaceX and Tesla that are aligned with his values. His commitment to his passions led to personal success and also contributed to advancements in technology and sustainability. By persisting through setbacks and challenges, Musk has shown the impact that can be made when one's actions are guided by their deepest values and interests. His dedication to his passions has not only driven him to success but has also inspired countless others to pursue their own dreams with similar determination. In a world full of uncertainties and obstacles, individuals like Musk and Mother

Teresa serve as shining examples of the incredible change that can be achieved through unwavering commitment to one's beliefs and goals.

In conclusion, identifying values and passions is essential for personal as well as professional fulfilment. By aligning our capabilities with what motivates us and brings us joy, we can find greater meaning in our endeavors and make a positive impact on the world. Whether it's pursuing a career that aligns with our values or dedicating ourselves to a cause we are passionate about, aligning values and passions leads to a fulfilling and successful life.

Identifying Values and Passions: A Key to Finding Meaning and Success in Life

What are values and passions, and why are they important? Values are the principles and beliefs that guide our decisions and actions and reflect what we consider important and worthwhile in life. Passions are the interests and hobbies that excite us, bring us joy, and reflect what we enjoy doing and learning about. When our values and passions are aligned, we feel fulfilled and satisfied in our personal and professional lives. This alignment can also increase motivation, productivity, and overall happiness. By identifying and pursuing our values and passions, we can create a life that is meaningful and successful on our own terms.

Values and passions are important because they:

Define our identity and personality and help us discover who we are and what we want to be.

Shape our goals and aspirations and help us determine what we want to achieve and how we want to contribute.

Influence our choices and behaviours and help in aligning our actions with our purpose and vision.

Enhance our well-being and happiness and help us find fulfilment and satisfaction in our endeavors.

Values and passions can vary from person to person, depending on their background, experience, and perspective. However, irrespective of the type of values and passions, they should be authentic and meaningful to us and not imposed or influenced by others.

How do you identify values and passions?

Identifying values and passions is the process of exploring and discovering what matters to us and what makes us happy. It is a key practice for everyone willing to live a meaningful and successful life.

Values and passions can be identified in various

ways, such as:

Reflecting and introspecting on our values and passions and asking ourselves questions that challenge us to think deeply and honestly about ourselves and our lives. Some examples of such questions are:

What are the things that I value most in life, and why?

What are the things that I enjoy doing the most, and why?

What are the things that I am good at, and why?

What are the things that I want to learn more about, and why?

What are the things that I want to achieve in life, and why?

What are the things that I want to change in the world, and why?

Exploring and experimenting with our values and passions and trying out new and different things that interest us and challenge us. We can use online or offline platforms to access and engage in various activities, such as:

Reading books, articles, blogs, or podcasts on topics that we are curious about or passionate about.

Taking courses, workshops, webinars, or coaching sessions on skills that we want to develop or improve.

Joining clubs, groups, communities, or networks that share our values or passions or offer opportunities to learn and grow.

Volunteering, mentoring, or donating for causes that we care about or support.

Traveling, visiting, or exploring places that we want to see or experience.

Seeking and receiving feedback from others who know us well or can offer us valuable insights and perspectives, such as our friends, family, mentors, or coaches. We can use formal or informal methods to solicit and obtain feedback, such as surveys, interviews, or conversations. We can also ask them questions that can help us identify our values and passions, such as:

What are the things that you think I value the most, and why?

What are the things that you think I enjoy doing the most, and why?

What are the things that you think I am good at, and why?

What are the things that you think I want to learn more about, and why?

What are the things that you think I want to achieve in life, and why?

What are the things that you think I want to change in the world, and why?

Identifying values and passions is essential to finding meaning and success in life. By exploring and discovering what is significant to us and what makes us happy, we can align our capabilities with our values and passions and pursue our goals and aspirations with passion and purpose. Whether it's finding a career that matches our values or finding a hobby that sparks our passions, identifying values and passions leads us to a fulfilling and successful life. When we are able to connect our actions and choices to our core values and passions, we are more likely to experience a sense of fulfilment and satisfaction in our daily lives. By understanding what drives us and brings us joy, we can create a life that is meaningful and purposeful. This alignment allows us to live authentically and make a positive impact on the world around us. Ultimately, by prioritizing our values and passions, we can lead a life that is truly fulfilling and successful.

It is important to regularly reassess our values and passions, as they may evolve over time. By staying true to ourselves and staying connected to what truly matters to us, we can continue to live a life that is aligned with our deepest desires and aspirations. This self-awareness and self-reflection can guide us in making decisions that are in line with our values and passions, ultimately leading to a more fulfilling and successful life. By prioritizing what matters to us in true sense, we can create a life that is rich in meaning and purpose, making a positive impact not only on ourselves but on those around us as well.

ATTRIBUTE F: TAKING ASSESSMENTS

Personality assessments, skills assessments, and career aptitude tests helps in understanding your strengths, preferences, and areas for potential development. These assessments might provide objective data to support your self-evaluation. They can also offer insights into potential career paths aligning with your interests and abilities. By taking these assessments, you can understand yourself in a better way and make more informed decisions for your future. They can serve as valuable tools for guiding your personal and professional growth.

Assessments are essential in the pursuit of personal and professional growth because they help people understand their strengths, preferences, and areas for progress. This practice is consistent with the Indian notion of "Jnana Yoga," which emphasizes self-awareness and comprehension as a path to enlightenment. By recognizing and acknowledging our strengths and weaknesses through assessments, we can work towards improving ourselves and reaching our full potential. This self-awareness enables us to set realistic goals and make decisions that align with our values and aspirations. Assessments are not just tools for understanding ourselves better but also for shaping our journey towards a fulfilling and successful life.

Several people in India have profited from undergoing evaluations. One such example is cricket legend Sachin Tendulkar. Tendulkar used assessments to better understand his batting tactics and limitations, allowing him to constantly improve his game to become one of the best cricketers of all time. By utilizing assessments, Tendulkar was able to pinpoint areas of his game that needed improvement and devise strategies to overcome them. This dedication to self-improvement and willingness to adapt based on assessments led to his immense success in the sport. Tendulkar's story serves as a powerful reminder of the transformative potential of self-awareness and the significance of utilizing assessments to reach our full potential in any endeavor.

Another example is Dr. A.P.J. Abdul Kalam, the former President of India. Dr. Kalam utilized assessments to understand his leadership style and areas for improvement, which helped him become an effective leader and inspire millions of people across nations.

On a global scale, companies like Google exemplify the importance of conducting assessments. Google uses assessments such as the "Googleyness" test to evaluate candidates' fit with the company's culture and values. This practice has helped Google build a highly effective and cohesive team of employees. By utilizing assessments, individuals and organizations can gain valuable insights that lead to personal and professional growth. Taking the time to understand strengths and weaknesses through assessments can lead to success and fulfilment in various aspects of life.

In conclusion, assessments play a crucial role in personal and professional growth. By obtaining insights into our strengths, preferences, and areas for improvement, we can make well-informed decisions regarding our careers and personal growth. Whether it is understanding our personality traits or identifying our skills and competencies, assessments can provide valuable data to supplement our self-evaluation and guide us towards success. Additionally, assessments can help individuals navigate career choices, as they can highlight areas where they excel and where they may need to improve. This self-awareness can lead to more satisfaction and productivity in the workplace. Moreover, assessments can also contribute to personal relationships by helping individuals understand their communication styles and emotional intelligence, leading to more meaningful connections with others. Overall, taking assessments is a valuable tool for self-discovery and growth in all areas of life.

Taking Assessments: How to Use Data to Enhance Your Capabilities and Achieve Your Goals

What are assessments, and why are they important? Assessments are tools and methods that measure and evaluate various aspects of our personality, skills, knowledge, or potential. They are important as they can assist us:

- Discover and understand our strengths and weaknesses and how we can leverage or improve them.
- Identify and explore our preferences and passions and how we can align them with our values and goals.

- Recognize and pursue our opportunities and challenges, and how we can overcome or learn from them.
- Compare and benchmark our performance and progress, and how we can improve or celebrate them.

Assessments can be of several types, such as personality assessments, skills assessments, or career aptitude tests, depending on the purpose and scope. However, regardless of the nature of assessment, it should be dependable, valid, and relevant to us, not biased or inaccurate. Furthermore, assessments should be conducted periodically to track our growth and development over time. We should remember that assessments are not meant to label us or limit our potential, but rather to provide valuable insight and feedback for personal and professional growth. By embracing assessments as a tool for self-discovery and improvement, we gain a deeper understanding of ourselves to make better decisions about our future endeavors. Assessments should empower us to confidently pursue our passions, overcome challenges, and celebrate our successes along the way.

How do you take assessments? Taking assessments is the process of accessing and completing various tools and methods that measure and evaluate our capabilities and potential. It is a key practice for people who want to improve themselves and achieve their full potential.

Taking assessments can be done in many ways, such as:

We can utilize online or offline platforms offering various assessments, such as websites, apps, books, or magazines. We can choose the assessments that suit our needs and interests and follow the instructions and guidelines to complete them.

seeking professional or expert guidance that can provide us with customized assessments, such as counsellors, coaches, or mentors. We can consult with them, share our goals and expectations, and receive their feedback and recommendations on the best assessments for us.

participating in formal or informal programs that require or provide assessments, such as courses, workshops, webinars, or interviews. We can enrol in or apply for these programs and complete the assessments as part of the curriculum or process.

How do I use assessments? Using assessments is a process of analyzing and applying the data and information that we obtain from various tools and methods that measure and evaluate our capabilities and potential. It is a crucial step for turning data into action and results.

Assessments can be done in many ways:

We can review and reflect on the data and information, and identify the key findings, insights, and implications. We can use a data summary or a data report to organize and present the data, or we can use data visualization or a data dashboard to display and analyze the data.

evaluating and prioritizing the data and information

and deciding which data to act on and which data to ignore. We can use a data criterion or a data scorecard to assess and rank the data, or we can use a data matrix or a data map to prioritize and classify the data.

Implementing and monitoring the data and information and taking concrete steps to enhance our capabilities and achieve our goals. We can use a data action plan or a data roadmap to outline and execute the data, or we can use a data tracker or a data dashboard to measure and track the data.

Taking assessments is essential for personal and professional growth. By utilizing various tools and methods that measure and evaluate our capabilities and potential, we can gain valuable data and information to supplement our self-evaluation. By analyzing and applying the data and information, we can enhance our capabilities and achieve our goals. Whether it is understanding our personality traits or identifying our skills and competencies, assessments can help us use data to improve ourselves and our lives. Utilizing tools like personality assessments or skills tests can offer valuable insights into areas where we excel and areas for improvement. This approach backed by data allows for targeted growth and development, leading to increased success and fulfilment in both personal and professional endeavors. For example, taking a personality assessment like the Myers-Briggs Type Indicator can provide insights into their communication style and how they interact with others. By understanding these traits, individuals can tailor their approach to work more effectively in team settings or leadership roles. This self-awareness and targeted development can lead to improved relationships and increased productivity in the workplace.

Furthermore, seeking feedback from colleagues and mentors can offer valuable insights into areas where improvement is needed. By actively soliciting feedback and taking constructive criticism to heart, individuals can continue to refine their skills and behaviours to become more effective and successful in their roles. Additionally, seeking out opportunities for further education and training can help individuals stay current in their field and continue to expand their knowledge and expertise. By taking an initiative-taking approach to personal and professional development, we can position ourselves for long-term success and fulfilment in our careers.

ATTRIBUTE G: SEEK LEARNING OPPORTUNITIES

Look for chances of continuous learning and growth. To get better at what you do, go to workshops, seminars, online classes, or professional development programs. Make sure you know about the latest developments and trends in your field. This continuous pursuit of knowledge will not only enhance your skills and expertise but also keep you competitive and relevant in today's fast-paced world. Remember that learning is a lifelong process, and by seeking out learning opportunities, you are investing in your future success. Stay curious, stay hungry for knowledge, and never stop seeking ways to improve yourself professionally and personally.

Looking for new things to learn is important for personal and career growth. In Indian culture, this theory fits with the idea of "Vidya," or knowledge, which is seen as a way to become wise and better yourself. By embracing the concept of "Vidya" and continuously seeking out new knowledge, you are not only expanding your own understanding and skills but also contributing to the betterment of society. So, whether you are learning a new language, taking up a new hobby, or pursuing a higher degree, remember that every bit of knowledge gained is a step towards a more fulfilling and successful future. Stay committed to your personal and professional development, and the rewards will surely follow.

There are many cases of people in India who have realized the importance of looking for ways to learn. Dr. B.R. Ambedkar, the architect of the Indian Constitution, serves as a prime example of this. Dr. Ambedkar went to college and became a famous professor, using his knowledge to fight for social justice and equality even though he faced many problems. Despite facing discrimination and adversity, Dr. Ambedkar's commitment to education and personal development allowed him to become a prominent leader in India's fight for social reform. His dedication to learning serves as an inspiring example of how continuous education can lead to impactful change and a more successful future.

Another example is Dr. A.P.J. Abdul Kalam, the former President of India. Dr. Kalam exemplified a lifelong learner who continuously sought opportunities to broaden his knowledge and skills. He considered learning as a lifelong process and encouraged others to do the same. Dr. Kalam's relentless pursuit of education and innovation led him to become a renowned scientist and visionary leader who played a key role in India's missile program. His belief in the power of education as a tool for personal growth and societal progress continues to inspire individuals worldwide to strive for excellence and make a positive impact on their communities.

On a global scale, individuals like Elon Musk exemplify the importance of seeking learning opportunities. Musk is known for his voracious appetite for reading and learning, which made him successful as an entrepreneur and innovator. He continuously seeks to expand his knowledge and stay ahead of industry trends, which has enabled him to lead companies like SpaceX and Tesla towards becoming successful.

In conclusion, seeking learning opportunities is essential for personal and professional growth. By continuously learning and staying updated with industry trends, we can enhance our skills and knowledge, adapt to changing environments, and achieve greater success in our endeavors. Whether it is attending a workshop, seminar, or online course, or simply reading a book, the pursuit of learning leads to new opportunities and enriches our lives. In today's fast-paced and competitive world, staying stagnant is not an option. By following in the footsteps of visionaries like Elon Musk, who prioritize continuous learning, we can position ourselves for success and growth. Embracing a learning mindset allows us to not only stay relevant in our current roles but also to explore new avenues and potential career paths. So, let us all commit to never stop learning and evolving, for the possibilities are endless when we are open to new knowledge and experiences.

Seeking Learning Opportunities: How to Enhance Your Capabilities and Achieve Your Goals

What are learning opportunities and why are they important? Learning opportunities are the several ways and means that we can access and acquire new skills and knowledge. They are important because they help us:

- Develop and improve our capabilities and increase our competence and confidence.

- Explore and discover new interests and passions and broaden our horizons and perspectives.

- Adapt and respond to changing situations and demands and increase our flexibility and resilience.

- Innovate and create novel solutions and products and increase our creativity and productivity.

- Advance and progress in our careers and lives and increase our opportunities and rewards.

Learning opportunities can be of several types, such as workshops, seminars, online courses, or professional development programs, depending on the format and content. However, irrespective of the nature of learning opportunities, they should be relevant, engaging, and effective for us, and not boring, irrelevant, or ineffective. By engaging in these learning opportunities, we can continue to adapt and grow in our personal and professional lives. It is important to seek out opportunities that challenge us and push us outside of our comfort zones in order to truly see growth and development. Remaining open to new opportunities and experiences, we can continue to advance and progress towards our goals and aspirations.

How to seek learning opportunities? Seeking learning opportunities is the process of actively looking for and finding ways and means to learn and grow. It is a key practice for everyone to improve themselves and achieve their full potential. One way to seek learning opportunities is to network with others from identical field or industry, as they may have valuable insights or resources to share. Additionally, taking on new projects or tasks at work that are outside of your usual responsibilities can help you gain new skills and knowledge. Seeking out workshops, seminars, or online courses related to your interests or career goals can also provide great learning opportunities. Overall, being proactive and curious about learning is essential to continue developing and growing personally and professionally.

Seeking learning opportunities can be done in several ways, such as:

- Utilizing online or offline platforms that offer various learning opportunities, such as websites, apps, books, or magazines. We can choose the learning opportunities that suit our needs and interests and follow the instructions and guidelines to access and complete them.

- Seeking professional or expert guidance that can provide us with customized learning opportunities, such as counsellors, coaches, or mentors. We can consult with them and share our goals and expectations and receive their feedback and recommendations on the best learning opportunities for us.

- Participating in formal or informal programs that require or provide learning opportunities, such as courses, workshops, webinars, or conferences. We can enrol or apply for these programs and complete the learning opportunities as part of the curriculum or process.

How to use learning opportunities? Using learning opportunities is the process of applying and integrating the skills and knowledge that we acquire from numerous ways and means of learning. It is a crucial step for turning learning into action and results.

Using learning opportunities can be done in numerous ways, such as:

- Reviewing and reflecting on the skills and knowledge, and identifying the key learnings, insights, and implications. We can use a learning summary or a learning report to organize and present the skills and knowledge, or we can use a learning journal or a learning portfolio to document and highlight the skills and knowledge.

- Evaluating and prioritizing the skills and knowledge and deciding which skills and knowledge to apply and which skills and knowledge to ignore. We can use a learning criterion or a learning scorecard to assess and rank the skills and knowledge, or we can use a learning matrix or a learning map to prioritize and classify the skills and knowledge.

- Implementing and monitoring the skills and knowledge and taking concrete steps to enhance our capabilities and achieve our goals. We can use a learning action plan or a learning roadmap to outline and execute the skills and knowledge, or we can use a learning tracker or a learning dashboard to measure and track the skills and knowledge.

Seeking learning opportunities is important for both personal and professional growth. By accessing and acquiring new skills and knowledge, we can enhance our capabilities and increase our competence and confidence. By applying and integrating the skills and knowledge, we can achieve our goals and make a positive impact on the world. Whether it is attending a workshop, seminar, or online course, or simply reading a book, seeking learning opportunities can enrich our lives and help us grow. Continuously seeking out new learning opportunities also allows us to stay relevant in a constantly evolving world. It enables us to adapt to changes in our industry and develop innovative solutions to challenges we may face. By taking the initiative to expand our knowledge and skills, we are investing in our future success and welcoming new possibilities.

Embracing a mindset of lifelong learning not only benefits us individually but also contributes to the betterment of society as a whole.

**EAT.
SLEEP.
HU$TLE.
REPEAT.**

**ATTRIBUTE : H
TACKING
PROGRESS**

ATTRIBUTE H: TRACKING PROGRESS

Keep an eye on your progress as time goes on. Review your goals and skills on a regular basis and make changes to your plans as needed. Celebrate the things you have done well and the places you have made progress. Remember to also acknowledge and learn from any setbacks or challenges you may face along the way. By tracking your progress and staying proactive in your self-improvement journey, you can stay motivated and continue moving forward towards your goals. Remember that personal growth is a journey, and every step, irrespective of how small, is a step in the right direction. Keep pushing yourself, and never forget to celebrate your achievements, big or small.

Keeping track of your success is important for

both personal and professional growth. It keeps you motivated and on track to reach your goals. From an Indian point of view, this theory fits with the idea of "Karma Yoga," which stresses the importance to act and check in with your efforts to make sure they are helping you reach your goals.

By staying mindful of your progress and actively working towards your goals, you are embodying the principles of Karma Yoga. It is about taking responsibility for your actions and continuously striving for self-improvement. By acknowledging your achievements, no matter how small, you are reinforcing positive habits and building confidence in your abilities. Remember, every step you take is a step towards growth and success. Keep moving forward with determination and dedication, and you will surely see the results of your hard work.

In India, there are many cases of people who have done better by keeping track of their progress. Ratan Tata, who used to be the head of the Tata Group, is a good example of this. Tata is known for taking an incredibly careful approach to business and keeping an eye on key performance factors to see how things are going. Tata Group has become one of India's biggest and most successful conglomerates by taking this method. Similarly, Indian cricketer Virat Kohli is also an example of someone who has achieved remarkable success by tracking his progress. Kohli meticulously monitors his performance statistics, fitness levels, and technique in order to constantly improve and stay at the peak of his game. This dedication to self-improvement has helped him become one of the best batsmen in the world and a successful captain for the Indian cricket team.

Another example is the Indian cricket team led by MS Dhoni. Dhoni was known for his calm demeanour and his ability to assess the team's performance objectively. By tracking their progress and adjusting as needed, Dhoni was able to lead the team to numerous victories, including the ICC World Twenty20 in 2007 and the ICC Cricket World Cup in 2011. Dhoni's commitment towards continuous improvement and strategic decision-making allowed the Indian cricket team to achieve success on the international stage. By maintaining a level-headed approach and analyzing performance data, Dhoni was able to lead his team to victory in key tournaments, solidifying their reputation as a dominating force in world cricket.

On a global scale, companies like Google exemplify the importance of tracking progress. Google uses data analytics to track user behaviour and measure the success rate of its products and services. This data-driven approach has helped Google continuously improve its offerings and maintain a competitive edge.

In conclusion, tracking progress is essential for personal and professional growth. By regularly reviewing your goals, assessing your capabilities, and adjusting your strategies as per the needs, you can stay focused and motivated towards achieving success. Whether it is celebrating your achievements or acknowledging areas where you have made improvements, tracking progress helps you stay on the path to success. Setting benchmarks and regularly monitoring your progress helps you in identifying areas of strength and areas for improvement. This self-awareness is crucial for personal development and can help you make informed decisions about your goals and priorities. By tracking your progress, you can also hold yourself accountable and stay committed to your objectives. Overall, tracking progress is a game-changing tool for growth and success in both your personal and professional lives.

Tracking Progress: A Guide to Measuring and Improving Your Performance and Outcomes

What is tracking progress, and why is it

important? Tracking progress is the process of monitoring and evaluating one's performance and outcomes over time. It is important as it can help:

- Stay on track and focused on one's goals and avoid distractions and deviations.
- Identify and rectify any gaps or challenges and find solutions or alternatives.
- Recognize and appreciate any achievements or successes and celebrate or reward oneself.
- Learn and grow from one's experiences, and apply the lessons learned to future endeavors.

Tracking progress can be done at various levels, such as individual, team, or organizational, depending on the scope and scale. However, regardless of the level, tracking progress should be done regularly and consistently, not sporadically or randomly.

How to track progress?

Tracking progress is the process of using various tools and methods to measure and evaluate one's performance and outcomes. It is a key practice for anyone willing to improve themselves and achieve their full potential. By tracking progress, individuals can identify what is working effectively and what requires improvement, allowing them to make the necessary adjustments and move forward. Setting specific goals and milestones can help guide the tracking process and provide a clear framework for success. Whether it be through journaling, data analysis, or regular check-ins with a mentor or coach, tracking progress is essential for personal and professional development.

Tracking progress can be done in various steps, such as:

Setting SMART goals and milestones and defining the indicators and criteria that will be used to measure and evaluate one's performance and outcomes. One can use a goal statement, a goal worksheet, or a goal contract to write and document one's goals and milestones, and a goal ladder, a Gantt chart, or a timeline to plan and schedule them.

Collecting and recording data and information and using various sources and methods to gather and document one's performance and outcomes. One can use a data collection tool, a data entry tool, or a data storage tool to collect and record one's data and information, and a data source, a data method, or a data quality tool to ensure the validity and reliability of one's data and information.

Analyzing and interpreting data and information and using various techniques and tools to process and understand one's performance and outcomes. One can use a data analysis tool, a data interpretation tool, or a data visualization tool to analyze and interpret one's data and information, and a data summary, a data report, or a data dashboard to organize and present one's data and information.

Evaluating and improving one's performance and outcomes and using various strategies and actions to enhance and optimize one's performance and outcomes. One can use a data evaluation tool, a data improvement tool, or a data optimization tool to evaluate and improve one's performance and outcomes, and a data action plan, a data roadmap, or a data tracker to outline and execute one's strategies and actions.

Tracking progress plays a key role in personal and professional growth. By measuring and evaluating one's performance and outcomes over time, one can identify one's strengths and weaknesses and find areas for improvement. By celebrating one's achievements and acknowledging one's improvements, one can remain motivated and inspired to achieve one's goals. Whether it is improving one's skills or increasing one's productivity, tracking progress can help one measure and improve one's performance and outcomes. For example, a student may use a study planner to track their progress on assignments and exams, allowing them to see where they may need to allocate more time or effort. By regularly updating and reviewing their study planner, the student can identify patterns in their study habits and adjust improve their academic performance.

This process of self-reflection and adjustment can also be applied to other areas of life, such as fitness goals or personal development. By tracking progress and making the necessary changes, individuals can grow and improve continuously in various aspects of their lives. Additionally, celebrating small victories along the way can provide a sense of accomplishment and motivation, thereby pushing forward towards larger goals. Overall, tracking progress is a valuable tool for staying focused, motivated, and achieving success.

BE PATIENT.

PROGRESS TAKES TIME.

ATTRIBUTE : I PATIENCE AND PERSISTENCE.

ATTRIBUTE I: PATIENCE AND PERSISTENCE

The Key Virtues for Personal and Professional Development

What are patience and persistence, and why are they important? Patience is about enduring difficulties and delays without losing calm and composure. Persistence is to continue pursuing one's goals and dreams despite obstacles and challenges. They are important because they can help one:

- Develop and improve one's capabilities and increase one's competence and confidence.
- Explore and discover one's interests and passions and broaden one's horizons and perspectives.
- Adapt and respond to changing situations and demands and increase

one's flexibility and resilience.

- Innovate and create innovative solutions and products and increase one's creativity and productivity.
- Advance and progress in one's career and life and increase one's satisfaction and happiness.

Patience and persistence are virtues that can be cultivated and practiced in various domains and aspects of one's life, such as personal, professional, academic, or social, depending on one's interests and goals. However, regardless of the domain or aspect, patience and persistence should be balanced and healthy, not excessive or unhealthy. Excessive patience can lead to missed opportunities and stagnant growth, while excessive persistence can result in burnout and frustration. Balancing patience and persistence is key to achieving success and fulfilment in all areas of life. By cultivating these virtues, individuals can navigate challenges, overcome obstacles, and reach their full potential.

How do you cultivate patience and persistence? Cultivating patience and persistence is all about developing and strengthening one's ability to endure difficulties and delays and to continue pursuing one's goals and dreams. It is a key practice for everyone who wants to improve themselves and achieve their full potential. Some ways to cultivate patience and persistence include setting realistic goals, breaking them into smaller tasks, and celebrating small victories along the way. It is equally important to practice self-care, such as getting enough rest, eating well, and managing stress effectively. By staying focused on the long-term benefits of perseverance and remaining committed to personal growth, one can build the resilience needed to overcome any obstacle that come along way. By embracing patience and persistence as core values, people can create a path to success and fulfilment in each area of their lives.

Cultivating patience and persistence can be done in various steps, such as:

Setting SMART goals and milestones and defining the expected difficulties and delays that one may encounter along the way. One can use a goal statement, a goal worksheet, or a goal contract to write and document one's goals and milestones, and a goal ladder, a Gantt chart, or a timeline to plan and schedule them.

Seeking learning opportunities and resources and finding ways and means to acquire and enhance the skills and knowledge that one needs to overcome or cope with the difficulties and delays.

One can use online or offline platforms to access and engage in various learning opportunities and resources, such as websites, apps, books, or magazines, or one can seek professional or expert guidance from counsellors, coaches, or mentors.

acting and implementing one's plans and taking concrete steps to overcome or cope with the difficulties and delays. One can use an action plan, a roadmap, or a tracker to outline and execute one's plans, and a progress report, a feedback loop, or a dashboard to monitor and measure one's progress and results.

reviewing and reflecting on one's outcomes and identifying the lessons learned, the achievements made, and the areas for improvement. One can use a learning summary, a learning report, or a learning portfolio to organize and present one's outcomes, and a learning journal, a learning matrix, or a learning map to analyze and interpret one's outcomes.

Cultivating patience and persistence is required for personal and professional growth. By developing and strengthening one's ability to endure difficulties and delays and to continue pursuing one's goals and dreams, one can unlock one is potential and discover hidden talents and capabilities. By learning from and growing from one's experiences, one can achieve one's goals and aspirations and find fulfilment and happiness. Whether it is pursuing a new career path, mastering a skill, or overcoming a personal obstacle, cultivating patience and persistence can help one achieve success and satisfaction in life.

Patience and persistence are key virtues on the journey of personal and professional growth. Developing capabilities is a gradual process that requires dedication and perseverance. From an Indian perspective, this principle resonates with the concept of "Saburi," which underscores the importance of patience and endurance during tough times. By embodying the principles of Saburi, individuals can navigate through life's obstacles with grace and resilience. During setbacks or delays, staying a positive and committed to one's goals can lead to eventual success. The combination of patience and persistence can pave the way for personal growth, self-discovery, and a sense of fulfilment in life.

In India, there are many people who have demonstrated the power of patience and persistence. One such example is Dr. APJ Abdul Kalam, the former President of India. Dr. Kalam faced many challenges in his early life but remained patient and persistent in pursuing his dreams. His hard work and dedication eventually led him to become one of India's most respected scientists and leaders. Despite facing financial struggles and limited resources, Dr. Kalam never gave up on his dream of becoming a scientist. Through hard work and perseverance for years, he eventually played a key role in India's missile development program and later became the President of the country. His story serves as a powerful example of how patience and persistence can lead to incredible success and personal fulfilment.

Another example is Mahatma Gandhi, who led India to independence through his unwavering commitment to nonviolent resistance. Gandhi's patience and persistence in adverse situations inspired millions of people across the world and led to significant social and political change.

Similarly, Marie Curie's dedication to scientific research and tireless pursuit of knowledge led to groundbreaking discoveries in the field of radioactivity, making her the first woman recipient of Nobel Prize. Her patience and persistence in the midst of scepticism and discrimination paved the path for subsequent generations of female scientists to pursue their passions and make important contributions to the world.

On a global scale, individuals like Thomas Edison exemplify the importance of patience and persistence. Edison famously said, "I have not failed. I have just found 10,000 ways that will not work," highlighting his resilience amidst failure. Edison's patience and persistence led to the invention of light bulb and numerous other innovations that have shaped the modern world.

Similarly, people like Rosalind Franklin and Marie Curie faced countless obstacles in their pursuit of scientific discovery, yet they remained steadfast in their commitment to their work. Curie's groundbreaking research on radioactivity and Franklin's crucial contributions to the understanding of DNA structure have had a long lasting impact on the fields of chemistry and biology. Their dedication serves as a powerful reminder of being perseverant in the face of adversity. In today's world, where challenges and obstacles abound, it is highly important than ever to embrace the qualities of patience and persistence in order to achieve our goals and make a positive impact on society.

In conclusion, patience and persistence are essential qualities for personal and professional growth. By staying committed to our goals and embracing setbacks as chances for learning and growth, we can overcome challenges and attain success. Whether it is pursuing a new career path, mastering a skill, or overcoming a personal obstacle, patience and persistence can help us in navigating the peaks and valleys of life with grace and determination. By embodying these qualities, we not only improve ourselves but also inspire those around us to do the same. As we face the uncertainties of the future, it is our patience and persistence that will guide us through the toughest of times and lead us towards a brighter tomorrow. So let us embrace these qualities wholeheartedly, knowing that they are the keys to unlocking our full potential and making a lasting impact on the world around us.

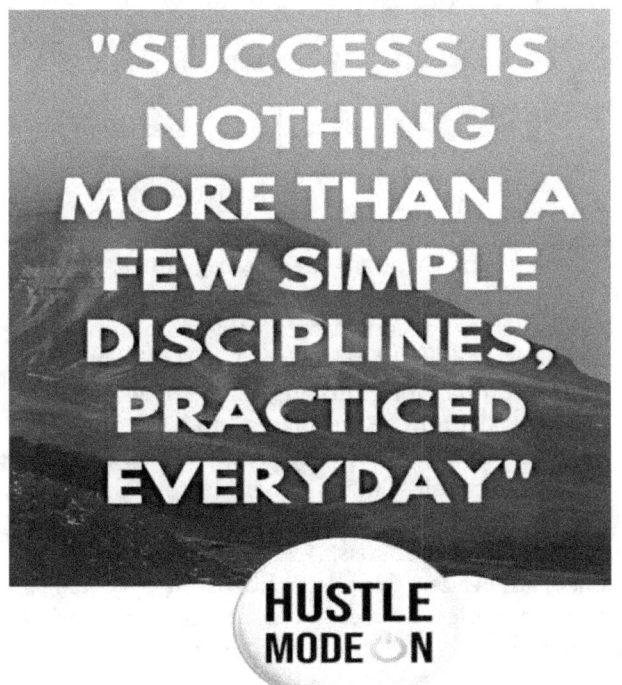

Other Book of the Author

Dr. Dibyendu Choudhury, one of India's eminent Management Gurus and mythologists, offers an interesting look at the top 25 personalities modern organizations may need in their leadership positions post pandemic. He draws on stories from the Mahabharata and the Ramayana. Businesses often need visionary leaders with an entrepreneurial spirit to steer them through challenging times. In the wake of the pandemic, most businesses don't know how to pick a leader who can successfully communicate, inspire workers, and strike the correct balance between strictness and compassion. This applies to any workplace i.e., Micro to Medium Enterprises and even large corporates. This is applied to any workplace. Dibyendu demonstrates the timeless management lessons that may be gleaned from stories written thousands of years ago. Be the Leader, Not the Boss! 25 Secrets to Being an Entrepreneurial Leader with Insights from Mythology draws on mythological figures and contemporary stories to reveal timeless truths about what it takes to be an effective and innovative leader. All his books available in

Amazon India Site.

India is a land of opportunities and challenges for anyone who wants to start or grow a business. With a population of over 1.3 billion, a diverse and dynamic market, a vibrant and innovative ecosystem, and a supportive and reform-oriented government. India offers immense potential for entrepreneurs and intrapreneurs alike. But doing business in India is not easy. It requires a deep understanding of the cultural, social, economic, legal, and political aspects of the country. To inspire you to pursue your dreams and aspirations with confidence and courage the Government Schemes and supports are mentioned as special features of this book.

This book is for you if:

-You are an entrepreneur who wants to start or scale up your business in India.
-You are an intrapreneur who wants to innovate or expand your existing business in India.
-You are a student or a professional who wants to learn more about the opportunities and challenges of doing business in India.
-You are NRI and want to return to India to start up your

venture.

In this book, you will learn:

-How to identify and validate your business idea or opportunity in India.

-How to create and execute your business plan or strategy in India.

-How to raise funds and manage your finances in India.

-How to build and lead your team and culture in India.

-How to market and sell your products or services in India.

-How to deal with customers, partners, competitors, regulators, and stakeholders in India.

-How to overcome the common pitfalls and problems of doing business in India.

-How to leverage the best practices and success stories of other entrepreneurs and intrapreneurs in India.

WEB REFERENCES

https://www.failory.com/startups/india-failures

https://startuptalky.com/expensive-mistakes-entrepreneurs-make/

https://www.hrfraternity.com/business-excellence/entrepreneurs-who-failed-before-succes-turning-setbacks-into-comebacks.html

https://aicontentfy.com/en/blog/importance-of-entrepreneurial-resilience

https://www.moneycontrol.com/news/trends/features/byjus-paytm-woes-rockstar-founders-need-to-accept-the-limits-of-theirpower-12241031.html

https://aaronhall.com/insights/the-power-of-embracing-failure-unlocking-success-and-growth/

https://insightbeforeaction.com/learn/digital-marketing-level-3/unit-208-understand-legal-regulatory-and-ethical-requirements-in-sales-and-marketing/

https://aicontentfy.com/en/blog/importance-of-building-strong-relationships-with-customers

https://intelligentmarketing.io/differentiating-markets-what-it-is-when-and-why-it-matters/

https://aaronhall.com/insights/resilience-adaptability-and-learning-keys-to-entrepreneurial-success/

https://aicontentfy.com/en/blog/overcoming-entrepreneurship-challenges-strategies-for-navigating-obstacles-and-thriving-1

https://www.amazon.in/How-Start-Business-India-Implementation/dp/B0CC5NGWR9

https://www.accelingo.com/apples-global-strategy/

https://hivo.co/blog/adaptive-moves-responsive-marketing-strategies-for-a-dynamic-market

https://aaronhall.com/insights/the-disruptive-visionary-jeff-bezos-leadership-style-and-amazons-success/

https://www.fixinc.io/resources/consequences-not-prioritizing-workplace-safety

https://aaronhall.com/insights/adapting-strategy-in-a-rapidly-changing-business-landscape/

https://aaronhall.com/insights/meeting-customer-needs-implementing-innovation-and-collaborating-for-success/

https://www.edtechdigest.com/2023/09/26/the-future-of-edtech-key-trends-shaping-the-landscape-in-2023-and-beyond/

https://www.linkedin.com/pulse/how-start-business-india-step-by-step-guide-rohit-okhera

https://www.latentview.com/blog/how-business-intelligence-can-help-you-with-better-decision-making/

https://paulfinchauthor.com/20-best-books-on-hindu-mythology-2023-reading-list-recommendations/

https://www.christianwalls.com/blogs/scripture-roundups/20-christian-podcasts-that-focus-on-leadership

https://indiacsr.in/csr-tcs-spends-rs-727-cr-in-social-development-programs-in-2022/

https://opensourcedworkplace.com/news/workplace/workplace-ethics-creating-a-culture-of-integrity-and-respect

https://www.linkedin.com/pulse/googles-25-year-journey-revolution-tech-history-awaynear

https://foundr.com/articles/building-a-business/be-your-own-boss

https://www.linkedin.com/pulse/embracing-change-adaptability-key-entrepreneurial-skill-remi-kuti-27wxe

https://finmark.com/startup-financial-planning/

https://infocoverage.com/popular-startups-in-india-that-shut-down-because-lack-of-funds/

https://news.harvard.edu/gazette/story/2022/01/helping-trapped-low-wage-workers-employers-struggling-to-fill-spots/

https://aaronhall.com/insights/innovation-and-differentiation-the-key-to-brand-success/

https://agmagency.com/not-everyone-is-your-customer-in-fact-most-people-arent/

https://buffer.com/resources/failure-entrepreneur-12-successful-entrepreneurs-tell-us-the-biggest-lessons-theyve-learned/

https://www.investopedia.com/articles/personal-finance/102015/series-b-c-funding-what-it-all-means-and-how-it-works.asp

https://www.linkedin.com/pulse/importance-financial-planning-management-workplace-jawad-salim

https://evangelize-consulting.com/2023/11/aligning-it-with-business-strategy-a-guide-for-cios/

https://marquee-equity.com/blog/how-to-build-a-network-of-advisors-and-mentors-who-can-help-you-navigate-the-fundraising-process/

https://www.linkedin.com/pulse/why-do-startups-fail-unpacking-top-7-reasons-failure-john-lee

https://aicontentfy.com/en/blog/awareness-tactics-how-to-engage-and-mobilize-target-audience

https://psychologily.com/finding-your-purpose/

https://startuptalky.com/shark-tank-india-impact-startup-ecosystem/

https://upqode.com/customer-feedback/

https://www.shopify.com/retail/word-of-mouth-marketing

https://www.oberlo.com/blog/how-to-be-your-own-boss

https://v.hdfcbank.com/htdocs/common/2022/july/Annual_Report_FY22/index.html

https://ecampusontario.pressbooks.pub/bio16610w18/chapter/turing-pharmaceuticals-a-glimpse-into-controversial-drug-pricing/

https://streamlynacademy.com/blog/a-detailed-zomato-case-study-2023/

https://www.ranktracker.com/blog/the-importance-of-trust-how-brand-credibility-drives-customer-loyalty/

https://wealthfactory.com/articles/protecting-personal-assets-from-business-liabilities/

https://biz.libretexts.org/Bookshelves/Business/Entrepreneurship/Book:_Entrepreneurship_and_Innovation_Toolkit_(Swanson)/01:_Chapters/1.01:_Chapter_1 Introduction_to_Entrepreneurship

https://businessmodelanalyst.com/zomato-business-model/

https://medium.com/thrive-global/not-everyone-is-your-customer-and-thats-ok-words-of-wisdom-with-christa-gurka-13084a8fee49

https://www.indiatimes.com/entertainment/originals/shows-like-shark-tank-india-to-watch-online-562093.html

https://www.socratic-method.com/quote-meanings/mahatma-gandhi-the-best-way-to-find-yourself-is-to-lose-yourself-in-the-service-of-others

https://www.mediabeacon.com/en/blog/case-study-social-understanding

https://www.linkedin.com/pulse/theranos-debacle-cautionary-tale-ambition-deception-power-elharony-igcef

https://raphaelreiter.medium.com/5-steps-to-a-happier-life-934ea048da0b

https://www.letsmastereverythingsimple.com/2024/02/leadership-lessons-from-dr-apj-abdul.html

https://www.forbes.com/sites/forbesbusinesscouncil/2024/03/29/ahead-of-the-curve-digital-transformation-in-marketing-and-events/

https://pulley.com/guides/startup-funding-rounds-series-a-b-c

https://www.oliandalex.com/meet-bmx-pro-morgan-wade-a-rising-star-in-extreme-sports/

https://www.linkedin.com/advice/0/how-can-self-reflection-help-you-set

https://www.lawinsider.in/columns/landmark-judgments-for-stay-on-execution

https://www.salon.com/2024/02/28/the-self-immolation-of-aaron-bushnell-should-serve-as-a-wake-up-call-for-the-military/

https://caclub.in/gst/rule-89-of-cgst-rules-2017-application-for-refund-of-tax-interest-penalty-fees-or-any-other-amount/

https://www.isc.hbs.edu/creating-shared-value/Pages/default.aspx

https://www.linkedin.com/advice/1/what-best-methods-creating-feedback-plan-skills-conflict-management

https://precisebusiness.com/catering-to-customer-needs/

https://www.wrike.com/blog/weekly-goals/

https://www.nbcnews.com/slideshow/road-sainthood-mother-teresa-advocate-poor-n642341

https://www.linkedin.com/pulse/importance-marketing-ethics-transparency-lessons-from-steven-brough

https://medium.com/@UrGirl/embracing-change-strategies-for-adapting-and-thriving-in-a-dynamic-world-f32de00d20b7

https://aaronhall.com/insights/the-power-of-goal-setting-achieving-growth-fulfillment-and-overcoming-challenges/

https://www.geeksforgeeks.org/essay-on-mother-teresa/

https://www.forbes.com/sites/benjaminlaker/2024/01/24/patience-unveiled-a-superpower-for-personal-growth-and-harmony/

https://www.msn.com/en-us/money/smallbusiness/byju-s-case-a-cautionary-tale/ar-AA1edKWU

https://www.tactyqal.com/blog/why-did-koinex-fail/

https://builtin.com/founders-entrepreneurship/series-a-startup-funding

https://en.wikipedia.org/wiki/

Tata_Consultancy_Services

https://www.mudra.org.in/

https://www.linkedin.com/advice/3/youre-evaluating-your-career-development-progress-h2bxe

https://www.linkedin.com/advice/0/how-do-you-use-feedback-from-multiple-sources

https://advisorycloud.com/blog/uncovering-the-secrets-of-elon-musks-success

https://welldoing.org/article/how-to-find-your-values-design-a-purposeful-life-around-them

https://time.com/5383389/google-history-search-information/

https://www.pressreader.com/ireland/new-ross-standard/20161129/281560880403052

https://www.workwithloop.com/blog/performance-testing-pitfalls-common-mistakes-and-how-to-avoid-them

https://shakespeare-online.com/plays/hamlet_1_5.html

https://www.forbes.com/sites/chriscarosa/2022/10/18/why-is-internal-locus-of-control-important-to-an-entrepreneur/

https://pib.gov.in/PressReleaseIframePage.aspx?PRID=1982867

https://udyamregistration.gov.in/Government-India/Ministry-MSME-registration.htm

https://medium.com/lampshade-of-illumination/the-role-of-self-reflection-in-personal-transformation-and-self-awareness-947f60092944

https://en.wikipedia.org/wiki/A._P._J._Abdul_Kalam

https://successindepth.com/action-verbs-for-smart-goals/

https://www.believeinmind.com/self-growth/importance-of-personal-values/

https://aaronhall.com/insights/redefining-success-the-key-pillars-for-a-fulfilling-life/

https://julienflorkin.com/self-improvement/personal-development/personal-growth/

https://www.leapsome.com/blog/continuous-performance-management

https://medium.com/pioneering-minds-in-physics/radiance-of-discovery-the-trailblazing-journey-of-marie-curie-e49c0c7d7985

https://www.linkedin.com/pulse/success-takes-time-embracing-perseverance-resilience- desiree-

https://medium.com/@michaeldejanna/overcoming-adversity-a-motivational-speech-to- ignite-your-inner-fire-b1f1608f74d7

https://www.indiascienceandtechnology.gov.in/listingpage/startup-grants-nidhi-programme

https://dayoneapp.com/blog/self-reflection/

https://www.sparknotes.com/philosophy/apology/mini-essays/

https://www.linkedin.com/advice/1/what-some-best-practices-soliciting-feedback

https://www.theguardian.com/science/2017/feb/15/india-launches-record-breaking-104-satellites-from-single-rocket112

https://medium.com/be-open/the-resilience-revolution-mastering-challenges-thriving-against-adversity-and-unleashing-your-57c2747f0077

https://zenguided.com/mindfulness-and-self-awareness/

https://en.wikipedia.org/wiki/MS_Dhoni

https://www.indiatimes.com/trending/human-interest/apj-abdul-kalam-missile-man-of-india-success-story-582124.html

https://historynewsnetwork.org/article/179504

About the Author

Dr. Dibyendu Choudhury

He currently lectures and trains a wide range of audiences, including professionals, aspiring business owners, business owners, and government officials.

Author of several academic articles and books on marketing and consumer behaviour; frequent business traveller; voracious reader; dedicated researcher; and, at heart, eternal student. He worked for various multinational corporations (MNCs) for extended periods in both India and other countries.

This book aims to provide relevant and contextual leadership lessons to those who are seeking them.

After the epidemic, he conducted interviews with real-world business owners, consultants, and service providers to learn more about the leadership gap and the qualities most in demand.

Websites to contact with the Author

www.dibyenduchoudhury.com
https://dibyenduchoudhury.academia.edu/

www.ingramcontent.com/pod-product-compliance
Lightning Source LLC
Chambersburg PA
CBHW071041240526
45471CB00014B/206